42 Financial Independence Laws For Christians

WHAT JESUS TAUGHT ME ON BECOMING RICH DURING COVID-19 & BEYOND

Ola Abina

Published by Jesus Is Too Real.

Baltimore, Maryland

www.jesusistooreal.com

Other Books By Ola Abina

Save Me From This Hour – How To Face Life's Adversities & Come Out Stronger

www.jesusistooreal.com. www.Olaabina.com

www.jesusistooreal.com

Praise For 42 Financial Independence Laws For Christians

"42 Financial Laws is a must have for every Christian NOW!"

– Megan Harrison

"Finally a practical Christian book on how to make and keep money."

– Frank Moller

"READ THIS BOOK for practical steps you can use now to become rich."

– Mike Smith

DEDICATION

I dedicate this book to my father, Dr. Elijah Abina who demonstrated in word and exemplary actions that Jesus is all you need to go from nothing to something.

Table of Contents

Acknowledgments

I would like to acknowledge the unflinching support and commitment of my wife, Odalisa, who is constantly paying the price of sharing her husband with the world. Her encouragement and efforts in allowing me to become what God has called me to be cannot be overemphasized. She is a true gem. I also appreciate my children Abisola, Mishael, Israel & Blessing, who have brought me so much joy. I sincerely cherish the support of my Senior Pastor, Pastor Taiwo Fagbuyi. He saw in me what I didn't see in myself and gave me the platform to express my giftings without reservations. Finally, to my Heavenly Father, the Son, and the Holy Spirit for committing to this earthen vessel the mystery of the Kingdom, and for the undeserved grace, unmerited favor, and mercy that sought and delivered a chronic sinner like me.

xiv

Introduction

"Just as the rich rule the poor, so the borrower is servant to the lender."

H i there. Perhaps you just took a peek to see what this book is about? Maybe this is what you have been looking for? It is even possible that the title of the book robs you off the wrong way? Oh, not again! Not another prosperity charlatan trying to steal people's money and lead them straight to hell. Don't people write about anything again these days? I can assure you that if you could take some time to read the rest of the entire book, you might probably agree that this book is urgently needed.

First, before I tell you a bit about my background, I believe every Christian ought to be rich. I believe that it is God's original plan for His people. Some may disagree, but I wholeheartedly believe that one of the reasons that Jesus came was to exchange our poverty for His riches. He wants Christians to be rich. He wants His followers to be rich. He wants YOU to be RICH! You would see if you read through this. One scripture that made this crystal clear is 2 Corinthians 8:9. *"You know the generous grace of our Lord Jesus Christ. Though he was rich, yet for your sakes* **he became poor, so that by his poverty he could make you rich."** This should be self-explanatory.

Some Christians believe this verse was referring to spiritual riches. However, that is not the case. When you look at the context in which this verse was written from the earlier verses, it was referring specifically to giving. Paul was talking about the giving of money.

*"Since you excel in so many ways—in your faith, your gifted speakers, your knowledge, your enthusiasm, and your love from us —I want you to excel also in this gracious act of giving."*2 Corinthians

You would notice that he already took care of the spiritual side of things but wants them particularly to succeed in giving as well. Let me add another bible verse also. 2 Corinthians 9:8, *"And God will generously provide all you need. Then you will always have everything you need and plenty left over to share with others."* This is also straight from God's word. I didn't add anything to it. That verse says God has the capacity to bless every Christian to the extent that they are never lacking on any occasion when giving of money is needed. Hmm...I believe God says what He means, and He means what He says.

God never intended for any Christian to be sick or be poor. It was all finished in Christ on the Cross of Calvary. God never intended for you to be poor. Now, are there Christians who are sick or poor? Yes. What this book intends to do is give practical financial steps for a Christian to get out of poverty and become rich. That includes you.

You say wait a minute. Is there an antecedent for this? Of course, in Deuteronomy 15:4. This is God addressing the children of Israel, preparing them for the Promised Land when He'd be their ruler. *There should be no poor among you, for the Lord your God will greatly bless you* in the land he is giving you as a special possession. Remember that Christians are the spiritual Jews, according to Galatians 3:29. *"And now that you belong to Christ, you are the true children of Abraham. You are his heirs, and God's promise to Abraham belongs to you."*

Ok. But did this actually happen? In the bible, yes. I will show you in a minute. Meanwhile, I had an all-night prayer session one night, and Jesus told me that Christians are not yet rich. Now, this runs contrary to popular opinions. The popular wisdom is that the church has too much money and is too rich. So, I asked why? He then pointed me to the wealth in the time of Solomon. He said that is the minimum standard of any people nation ruled by God. See for yourself.

*"The **king made silver and gold as plentiful in Jerusalem as stone.** And valuable cedar timber was as common as the sycamore-fig trees that grow in the foothills of Judah."2 Chronicles 1:15.*

*"All of King Solomon's drinking cups were solid gold, as were all the utensils in the Palace of the Forest of Lebanon. They were not made of silver, **for silver was considered worthless in Solomon's day!** I Kings 10:21.*

Good enough. Would every Christian be rich? It depends on the Christian. God has His responsibilities, and so does the Christian. I have this book for the Christian who wants to be rich.

A little bit of my background. I am passionately committed to the cause of Christ. I have a close relationship with Jesus. He has appeared to me several times and talks to me about specific things, ideas, companies, politics, things past, present and future, etc. Jesus is more important to me than money. I view any money that comes into my hand as a tool to win souls to Jesus. I want to be able to use my resources to bring at least 1,000,000 people to Jesus every year so that they can know that He is too real. I also want every Christian to be rich. There is an assault from the devil on Christians not to be rich.

My experience has spanned many areas of endeavors from corporate America, to the U.S. military, oil and gas, real estate, e-commerce, equities (stocks), cryptocurrencies, fine arts, publishing, pre-ipo, billboard advertising, etc.

I know what it is to be poor and suffer from great lack. Without money, Christians will not be able to do what Jesus commanded us to do. We will always be at the mercy of the world. We will lack an economic voice. Just look at what you are unable to do because of lack and money and add this to the list. However, with wealth in every Christian household, we are limitless.

Many Christians know the laws of nature and obey them. They know the spiritual laws and obey them. They know how to read the bible, fast and pray but don't know how to make a connection between wealth promised in the bible and bringing them into reality. There are financial laws that govern money. They have no respect of persons, whether Christians or Satanists. Whoever obeys these laws wins the money game!

The financial laws that I discussed in this book were taught to me either directly as verbal communication, through visions, spirit implantation, through life experiences, expanded reading and studying and prayers by the Lord Jesus. They are backed up with practical testimonial proofs and scriptural references of their effectiveness.

The laws applied correctly could lift you from poverty to financial independence. As a Christian, you need to solve the money challenge. It is not the will of God for you to be working several jobs and have no time to train your children because money is not enough. That means Satan has won the battle for your children.

Pain inspired me to write this book. I have seen many Christians put to shame because of lack of money. I heard the story of an anointed young Pastor whose life could have been saved for just $26,000. I cried to God for many days on this. Our Father is the Maker of the universe. We are heirs. We should not live like paupers.

A plus for this book is that I provided the "how tos" for you to be able to take practical steps to become rich. I provided website resources for steps you can take immediately.

*Disclaimer: Nothing in this book constitutes financial advice. It is for educational and informational purposes only. This book is meant to transform, spark and desire to reach out for more of God.

It is written with the intent that disciples of Jesus Christ (Christians) would be able to break free from financial lack, poverty and demonstrate to the world that Jesus paid the price for us to become rich!*

PART I:
FUNDAMENTAL LAWS

I n this part of the book, we will discuss the fundamental financial laws, which are the basic building blocks on which riches rest. I will show you what to put in place as Jesus taught me that should prevent your financial house from tumbling down.

CHAPTER 1

LAW OF CHANGE

"For everything there is a season, a time for every activity under heaven." Ecclesiastes 3:1.

Wwhen changes happen, transfer of wealth occurs. The community or the world at large would move from one form to another when changes happen. Many people are reluctant to embrace change. Ironically, embracing and positioning yourself with the financial law of change is required for you be rich.

You desire to change from being broke, or financially stranded don't you? Then a change must take place. Change of mindset, perspective, habits, association etc. Some things must change in your life if you want to become rich. You must be able to embrace the change around you.

As at the time of this writing, because of the COVID-19 pandemic, the world is in a terrible situation than we have ever witnessed in our lifetime. Lots of problems abound. If you read the latest headlines, you'd find that the Gross Domestic Product (GDP), which is the total of the value of all goods and services produced in an economy for many countries, have taken a huge hit. Singapore's had plunged by 62% and that of the U.S. by 32%. Many people have been laid off, out of money, out of work. The U.S. unemployment rate is at an all-time high of 14.70%. Several bellwether stores that have been around for ages are now filing for bankruptcies. Small businesses are not spared either. The future and system of doing work is gradually being changed from one form to the other, especially regarding physical presence.

Since we are in unusual times, there are some things we must know regarding where we work and earn income since it impacts us. We must know that employers are not in the business of making us comfortable, giving us pay increases, taking care of our healthcare, or providing a good retirement package for us. Those things are noble and should be done. However, that was not the driving force for starting businesses from the business owners' point of view. A business generally is started for profit. Profit is the reason why a business owner starts a business. That is why employees could be laid off regardless of their loyalty to the business or how long they have been working for the company.

You might have heard that some businesses got loans from the Payroll Protection Program from the government and still fire their workers. Surprisingly, the loan was for keeping employees on the payroll. It lets employees know that a business owner has different priorities.

There are many jobs that have been lost because of the pandemic and would never come back. Perhaps yours is one of them? As I mentioned earlier, the pandemic has changed the nature and future of work. If you also noticed in the U.S., there is a shortage of change for cash. Customers are being told to come with the exact amount to pay for goods. The world is gradually transitioning to a cashless society.

Even now, many businesses are installing more self-service and automated machines, replacing the need for human beings. Many big-name companies that have been around for years are filing for bankruptcy.

Now, if you look at all the above, it is easy to conclude that everything is all doom and gloom. Until you read headlines such as Jeff Bezos, the CEO of Amazon, made $13 billion on Monday, July 20, 2020, Elon Musk, the CEO of Tesla $8bn on Monday, August 17th, 2020, or that 36-year-old Mark Zuckerberg of Facebook is now worth over $100 billion.

A deeper dive into why, in the same economy, when some are making the most money they have ever made, others are losing the most they have ever lost, speaks volumes. Minimally, it shows that the folks that I mentioned earlier had positioned themselves for the change by embracing the financial law of change.

I would not dwell too much on this for now, but just as a form of background into the necessity of change. This means, in the simplest form, that all hope is not lost for us. We should not dismiss this as just another headline or complain as we used to. The truth is that there are opportunities for increasing our income during this pandemic than ever before. I will discuss specifically what Jesus told me about this in the Law of Embracing Technology.

Action Item.

1. What would I do if I was fired by my employer today?

2. I must prepare for change.

3. I must know that change is inevitable.

CHAPTER 2

LAW OF THE RICH BECOMING RICHER & THE POOR POORER

"To those who use well what they are given, even more will be given, and they will have an abundance. But from those who do nothing, even what little they have will be taken away." Matt. 25:29

The surprising financial law that Jesus taught me, which might have many people up in arms, is the law of the rich become richer and the poor becoming poorer. Some may say, but Jesus said in Matthew 26:11 that *"you would always have the poor among you."* That is true. Let me clear this up. God does not intend for anyone to be poor, neither did He want the poor to be poorer. This is one of those situations where you consider the original plan of God versus reality. The original plan of God was for every one of His children to be rich. He said in Deuteronomy 15:4 while making a covenant with the children of Israel, which is a foreshadow of the life of modern-day Christians that, *"There should be no poor among you, for the Lord your God will greatly bless you in the land he is giving you as a special possession.* The reality is that many of God's children,

5

Christians are poor.

There is also a common misconception that God wants everyone to be equal financially. This mentality is also false and runs contrary to the scripture. Are we commanded to help the poor and those who don't have? Yes. Must this be forcefully taken? No. Should those who lack have a sense of entitlement that they deserve what they didn't work for? No. As long as you believe and operate with the mentality that the rich or anyone that has more than you is obligated to give you something simply because they have more than you, then you should prepare for a life of poverty.

There ought to be no one who is a child of God who is poor. In some cases, people fall into poverty, maybe through no fault of their own. Maybe they were hit by a medical condition that wiped them out. However, in many cases, it is the actions of the poor that make them poorer. That is why the theme of this book rides on Jesus' promise to Christians in 2 Corinthians 8:9, *"You know the generous grace of our Lord Jesus Christ. Though he was rich, yet for your sakes he became poor, so that **by his poverty** **he could make you rich**."*

Again, the bible tells us that God is able to make you and I to have more than enough financially in 2 Corinthians 9:8 *"And God will generously provide all you need. Then you will always have everything you need and plenty left over to share with others."* Notice that it didn't say God may. It says, *"God will generously provide...plenty left over."* Read both scripture verses again and again until you believe it is for you and possible with you.

Now that the above is settled, let's settle down to take the law apart and see why. In the story of the parable of the talents, Jesus taught us this law of the rich getting richer and the poor poorer. We will examine it through this parable.

Our Lord Jesus told a story which we refer to as the Parable of the Talents in Matt 25:14-30 that drove this point home. He told us of a man going on a journey who then called his three servants and gave five talents, two talents and one respectively. The person given five talents traded with it and return with additional five making a total of ten talents. The servant with two talents also deployed the talents, gained two additional to make four. The story was different from the servant with one talent. While naturally, many would have thought that this would be the easiest to manage and deploy having only just one, the servant saw it differently. The perspective of the servant was that he got the short end of the stick. In fact, he accused the Master of being cruel and wicked because he only gave him one talent. The master, according to him, ought not to have expected any profit in return.

Do you not feel the same as this servant with only one talent? How many times have you always fantasized or complained that if only you had a special gift like someone else or born into opulence, things would have been different? Only if you had been born in the U.S. or attended college, know programming, etc.

Meanwhile, to the amazement of Jesus's listeners, the master was furious and did not agree with the lazy servant's assessment. Contrarily, he took his sole talent and gave it to the servant who had ten talents making him richer. He originally had five and had gained five more. While he banished the lazy servant to punishment, the conclusion was that even that person that thought what they had was not enough, got that taken from them and given to the rich.

In many places that you may look today, you would notice protests against the rich. Many people are upset and angry that the rich are getting richer. They believe they have gotten too much. Others even think that what is in the hand of the rich should be forcefully taken and redistributed to the poor. You must know and understand the law of the rich becoming richer and the poor poorer and use this to your advantage. This is one of the reasons the folks I mentioned earlier are getting richer while the poor are getting poorer. They are obeying these laws. Granted, there are some individuals who have ill-gotten wealth. That is not those we are referring to according to this law.

Regrettably, the wealthy are building businesses, creating enterprises where the poor go to shop. This returns the money back again into the coffers of the wealthy, making them wealthier and the poor poorer? You are making someone rich every day with the choices you make. Why not you?

The principle of the rich getting richer is biblical. A rich or wealthy person who obtained their wealth through moral means, of course, is rewarded by the principles God has put in place to become richer. The poor, on the other hand, who failed to use what he has would become poorer. God is a shrewd businessman. He expects returns whenever He invests. He has no sympathy for those who fail to use their gifts to generate returns.

Do you want an example of a five-talent person in our contemporary world making good use of their talent? Jeff Bezos of Amazon. He started with selling books. Now you find virtually everything on Amazon. I cannot possibly mention everything he has but here are others: Amazon Web Services (Cloud), Whole Foods (Grocery Store), Blue Origin (Spaceship), The Washington Post (Media), Zappos (Shoes), etc. I have posted a visual representation below. While looking at it, picture what impact a Christian could make in our world with such ventures, especially in bringing others to the knowledge of our Lord Jesus Christ? That is a lot of souls to the kingdom of God. Guess what? It is possible for you and me!

Did you notice that during the pandemic, many wealthy folks are making insane amounts of money more than they had made in their entire lives while for others, it is directly opposite? My goal for Christians reading this book is that you will be in this group by applying these laws to your advantage. If you are poor and despise the rich, chances are you'd never become one. What you resent, you cannot experience.

Action Item.

1. What talents have I been given by my Creator?

2. I need to have a different mindset that doesn't blame the rich for my problems.

3. I need to evaluate where I am making someone else rich and see what opportunities I could take advantage of.

4. I need to use this law to my benefit.

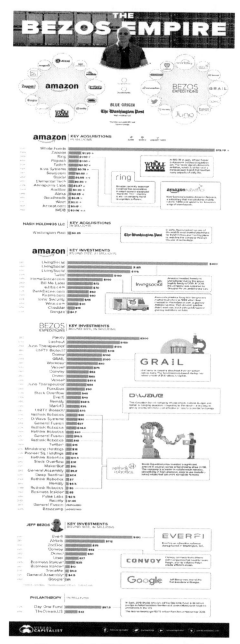

Figure 1. Jeff Bezos' Empire[1]

CHAPTER 3

LAW OF HARD WORK

"...It's a good thing when you're young to stick it out through the hard times." TM. Lamentations 3:27.

Have you ever wondered or thought about how fortunate life would have been if you had been born into opulence? Hmm…How about let's say you were born into the family of the Monarchs of England? Or if you had been born into the family of successful business owners like the Johnson & Johnsons or Waltons of Walmart, Hiltons of Hilton hotels? Maybe you had fantasized that if you had just been a bit as smart as Bill Gates. Or thought what if you had gotten some of the "lucky breaks" the rich in the world had gotten, your life, at least financially, would probably have turned out quite different? I have. I have thought about what it would be to live and not have money worries in the world.

While the path to riches for everyone is different, for the majority it runs through hard work. Often, you mismanage what you don't work hard for.

Jesus taught me through many practical experiences that there is no substitute for hard work in becoming rich, especially if you are starting from ground zero. *"Despite their desires, the lazy will come to ruin, for their hands refuse to work." Proverbs 21:25.* Not even the anointing of God, on one's life would substitute for hard work.

There are several dozen scriptures that I can give regarding hard work. Before Isaac became very rich, he worked hard, persistently sowing in his fields when there was nothing to show for it. He gave up and wanted to go to Egypt, but God instructed him to stay put in Gerar (Genesis 26). He obeyed and didn't get results till the end of the year. Your end of the year may not be the literal December 31st, but I can assure you in the name of Jesus, that you will succeed if you don't give up. Jacob also worked very hard for 20 years, some of which he was defrauded. However, he left with great riches at the end (Genesis 31). *"So let's not get tired of doing what is good. At just the right time we will reap a harvest of blessing if we don't give up." Galatians 6:9.*

I remembered launching into e-commerce. It was hard work. Probably over a thousand hours of watching instructional videos and paying thousands of dollars in courses and mentorship. I wasn't profitable at the initial stages as I learned and put into practice what I had learned. I lost thousands of dollars, but I continued to be resolute. Many times I would stay up for more than 24 hours working on my online store. I would be setting up the store, working on videos for marketing, advertising on various social media platforms. Said goodnight to my wife and kids while they go to bed, only for them to wake up and find me still working. Still, I will be praying to God that this is too much. Help me! I was kicking and kicking. Praying and fasting. I still had to prepare sermons to preach in church, find time to be a husband to my wife, father to my kids in playing with them, lead the choir and other departments in church, and oversee my other sources of income, as well as read and research for my paid employment. The Lord Jesus said, *"But Jesus replied, "My Father is always working, and so am I." John 5:17.*

Many of the rich billionaires that you see today worked hard at the initial stages of their ventures. This is what Bill Gates had to say. *"I didn't believe in weekends; I didn't believe in vacations; I mean, I knew everybody's license plate so I could tell you over the last month when their car had come and gone from the parking lot...But yes, I have a fairly hardcore view that there should be a very large sacrifice made during those, those early years, particularly if you're trying to do some engineering things that you have to get the feasibility."* [2]

This quote is from Jeff Bezos the current richest man in the world ($193.5 billion). *"You get certain gifts in life, and you want to take advantage of those,"* Bezos said during a 2017 Q&A at Seattle's Museum of Flight. But working hard at what you're good at? *"That's a choice,"* says Bezos. For example, *"you might be really good at math; it might be really easy for you. That's a kind of gift,"* Bezos said. *"But practicing that math, and taking it to the next step, that could be very challenging and hard, and take a lot of sweat."* [3]

Do not substitute the time to work on your business with just prayers and the word all day long. Just as much as you labor or work hard in reading the bible and prayer, you must also work hard in your business or vocation. No one can do it for you. For example, no matter how anointed you are, if you are married, you cannot ask God to love your spouse for you. You must do that. It is the same thing regarding work hard. I heard this quote from my Pastor. "Work hard as if it all depends on working hard. Then pray as if it all depends on prayer." I believe that it is a good maxim to live by. I also love this quote from Ray Pritchard, which I think summarizes everything. *Hard work yesterday does not guarantee tomorrow's success. Hard work yesterday has to be followed up with hard work today to guarantee tomorrow's prosperity.* [4]

Being a Christian, God's anointing would not and cannot take the place of hard work. Look at these scriptures. This is straight from God's word. It doesn't get better than these.

" I walked by the field of a lazy person, the vineyard of one with no common sense. I saw that it was overgrown with nettles. It was covered with weeds, and its walls were broken down. Then, as I looked and thought about it, I learned this lesson: A little extra sleep, a little more slumber, a little folding of the hands to rest— then poverty will pounce on you like a bandit; scarcity will attack you like an armed robber."
Proverbs 24:30

Action Item.

1. Determine to work hard at my craft.

2. I need to pick up again that dream that I left off and work harder.

3. I need to do all I can do so God can do all He can do.

4. Every week, I need to watch at least three videos and read two stories of those working in my industry and other fields who succeeded despite the odds.

CHAPTER 4

LAW OF GREAT RISKS FOR GREAT REWARDS

> "Send your resources out over the seas; eventually you will reap a return. Ecclesiastes 11:1" Complete Jewish Bible.

Another financial law that Jesus taught me is that it takes great risk to produce great rewards. Many Christians want to have great riches but don't want to take any risk at all. To have great riches, you must take big financial risks. This means if you intend to become rich, you must prepare to take risks.

The bible says this, *"Send your resources out over the seas; eventually, you will reap a return." Ecclesiastes 11:1. Complete Jewish Bible.* To understand this scripture, you need to understand that in biblical times, kings send sailors to go around the world and trade. Solomon, the writer of Ecclesiastes, did this. *2 Chronicles 8:18. "Hiram sent him ships commanded by his own officers and manned by experienced crews of sailors. These ships sailed to Ophir with Solomon's men and brought back to Solomon almost seventeen tons[a] of gold."* While Solomon's endeavor ended positively, it is not always a happy ending for everyone. For example, King Jehoshaphat also built a fleet of ships to sail to Ophir for gold, but it ended with disaster. They could not even leave the port.

Risk implies that there is a possibility of loss because your resources would be exposed to danger. There is also a possibility of a reward. All through the ages, only those who stepped out to take great risks are compensated with great rewards. For example, when David was to face Goliath, King Saul promised whoever defeats Goliath a great reward, his daughter in marriage and tax exemption for his family (I Samuel 17:25). Goliath is about nine feet tall! He has been a warrior practically all his life. No one in Israel was a match for him. But young David stepped forward. The first thing he asked was what was the reward to be given to anyone who defeats Goliath? He sees the risk, but he is more motivated by the reward.

For you to become rich applying this law, the rewards must significantly outweigh the risk. Also, only take an informed risk. Don't risk where you don't have the competence or can't acquire the required knowledge. In Solomon's example above, he took a great risk sending ships overseas to trade gold, and it paid off handsomely. This was only possible because he acquired external competence. He partnered with King Hiram, who has experienced sailors.

In contemporary times, although it is more common now for many young folks to drop out of college, start a company in a garage, and then a few years build a successful company, when Bill Gates dropped out, it wasn't so. Going to college in his time and even now guarantees a surer path to success. Dropping out to build a company that no one could predict the outcome is not. Fortunately, forty-five years after he founded Microsoft, he is the second richest person on the planet.

If you want to become rich, this is one financial law that is not optional. The path to riches runs through the valley of risks. When Jesus told us in the bible of the parable of the talents, found in Matthew 25:30, the reason the last servant failed to invest was because he was afraid of taking a risk. *"I was afraid I would lose your money, so I hid it in the earth. Look, here is your money back."* Matthew 25:25.

You should not be afraid of taking risks. I recommend the following regarding taking financial risks: Seek Jesus's direction or opinion on the matter. Once you clear it with Him, go ahead and start getting as much information as you can on the matter. Ask lots of questions until you are comfortable. Analyze the opportunity properly. Make sure the time frame, management, partner or vendor are thoroughly vetted. Don't just take their word for it no matter how close you are.

One of the mistakes I made in the past was transferring the trust of a trusted friend to the business associate that they brought. I lost a considerable amount on that investment. Don't do that. Treat everyone introduced to you by any trusted party as a complete stranger and let them earn your trust through the extensive process on their own. There is no guarantee that it would be smooth sailing at the initial stages. However, if Jesus led you there, stay there. It would work out one hundred percent of the time.

I have taken risks and still continue to take financial risks in Pre-Initial Public Offering opportunities for companies not yet trading publicly and other private placement opportunities. I must say that I took those risks at Jesus's direction.

Obeying God is also taking a risk. Faith is taking risks. You believe and listen to the direction of the person you don't see. The story that I shared in later Chapter 17 of when Jesus told me to empty my account and give to some servants of God was a huge risk. I either believe it was from Him or not. He never told me what the result would be. I only trusted him. Thank God the reward has more than compensated for the risk.

Action Item.

1. Thoroughly evaluate investment opportunities that I come across.

2. Seek Jesus's direction.

3. Get more information enough to be comfortable.

4. Vet everyone involved. Ask lots of questions.

5. I must know that no deal is do or die.

CHAPTER 5

LAW OF BUDGETING

*"Then Pharaoh should appoint supervisors over the land
and let them collect one-fifth of all the crops during the
seven good years. Have them gather all the food produced
in the good years that are just ahead and bring it to
Pharaoh's storehouses. Store it away, and guard it so there
will be food in the cities. That way there will be enough
to eat when the seven years of famine come to the land
of Egypt. Otherwise, this famine will destroy the land."*
Genesis 41:34-36.

F ew years ago, my small church of just about 200 at the time held a mortgage burning service. We paid off our 30-year mortgage of almost $700,000 on a four and a half-acre property in five years. Prior we had been in debt. We were broke. Our total debt profile was just a few dollars shy of $1,000,000, but in a few years, things had turned around. In addition to crying to God for help, we implemented budgeting. On the day of the mortgage burning service, while in prayer, the Lord told me to follow the same principle of budgeting that the church had followed if I want to be debt-free and wealthy.

Budgeting is simply telling your money where you want it to go. Money has this funny attitude that if you don't tell it where to go, it would get lost in the wrong hands. It would miss its way home. If you don't have plans for your money, you can be sure others do. Once you get paid, right on your phone, you would be bombarded with different advertisements for "buy me" the moment you are paid. If you had given instructions ahead to your money, which you stick to, your money would not get lost.

In Genesis 41:34-36, Joseph recommended the financial law of budgeting to Pharaoh. This was what saved Egypt during the worldwide famine. *"Then Pharaoh should appoint supervisors over the land and let them collect one-fifth of all the crops during the seven good years. Have them gather all the food produced in the good years that are just ahead and bring it to Pharaoh's storehouses. Store it away, and guard it so there will be food in the cities. That way there will be enough to eat when the seven years of famine come to the land of Egypt. Otherwise this famine will destroy the land."*

In order to live a financially independent life, a Christian must master the law of budgeting. It allows you to bring giving, saving, investing and spending into balance. You need to know how much income you are making, what you are spending (expenses), and what you could afford to keep (save), give and invest.

Some are naturally gifted in bringing into perfect harmony what they earn, spend, save, give and invest just as you are naturally gifted in other things. However, for the rest of us, we have to rely on what is called a budget. I know it is a dreaded word that some avoid. The reason why some are thrown off when the word budget is mentioned is that they are not able to keep to it. For others, they see no path to financial independence and accordingly disregard budgeting.

Even so, being financially independent or rich would cost you something. Let me put it this way. It's possible that you may not like where you are currently working. Yet you must go to that job to get paid so that you can eat, pay for shelter, clothes, buy medications, etc. No one would really give you a substantial amount of money for free for your keep continuously. You would have to work for it. Since this is already settled, I would like you to use that motivation of dissatisfaction with your current financial situation to put in a little time to find out what you are earning, how you are spending it, and how you can save, invest and give.

There are several ways to budget. You could do the old-fashioned way. Get about four envelopes and label them Savings, Expenses, Investment and Giving. Then you distribute the money you have earned into these envelopes. There are also tools available for free online. Look for what you are comfortable with and do it. Goodbudget.com provides a traditional envelope on a digital platform approach. Mint.com and PocketGuard.com allows you to budget at account level. It connects to your accounts and lets you know if you are overspending in any area since it gets information about what you are spending automatically from your account. As with every other company recommended in the book, it is at your risk. I recommend doing your own due diligence first. I have no affiliation with any of them and do not get compensated in any way from them. The most important thing is being comfortable with whatever budget method you choose and sticking to it. If you don't want to go the app route, plug your income and expenses into an Excel spreadsheet. You could also just get a calculator, a book, a pen and write what you earn, what you spend, room to give and save.

"The wise have wealth and luxury, but fools spend whatever they get."

Cutting Spending & Expenses

To save, you must critically look into you what you spend your money on, cut out anything that is not essential to your living. Food and shelter are just about the most common. Now, if you are spending too much on food or shelter, it needs to be reduced. If you can't find anywhere at all to save, then you will need to find a way to earn extra income. That extra would go straight into savings after, of course, paying tithes. Also, since you believe that God would make you greater financially, it is not a bad idea to set yourself up with a system so that when the blessing increases, there is room to contain it. If you tried budgeting, cutting expenses, saving and failed, it is natural and normal. I did it several times. The key is to keep getting back up each time and again.

Long-Term Savings

Have you ever come across some golden opportunities that you couldn't take advantage of, maybe a property on fire sale or other once in a lifetime opportunities that you weren't able to do because of lack of funds? Do you know that God orchestrated those to transfer wealth to you, but you were not prepared? That is one of the reasons to have long-term savings.

You must strive to save something. I would recommend after looking at what your total income is, save at least ten percent of what you make. This should be at least your floor level. Remember, the Lord only requires you to pay ten percent off the gross of your income as tithes. You should save at least ten percent as a way of rewarding themselves for the energy and time put in to earn the income. Pay yourself first, then pay others. If you are paid via direct deposit, set aside ten percent to always go to another account that you don't have an ATM card to, which is probably on the far side of town that would require extra effort to get to. If you are given an ATM card by the bank, cut it in two. Don't get checkbooks. Deposit the money in the most restrictive account you could find.

Short-Term Savings

This savings is different from the ten percent that comes off the top of your income for long-term savings. Sometimes you need funds for other short-term things that you want to do. It could be for going to the movies or taking your spouse out on a date. It could be a quick road trip. A weekend getaway. You could use your short-term savings for these. Any short-term needs could fall into your short-term savings.

How can you fund your short-term savings? I will give you some ideas. One method that may work is withdrawing in cash money allocated for items such gas, food and other regular consumables and putting them in envelopes clearly marked **SHORT-TERM EXPENSES**. Also, get another envelope labeled **SHORT-TERM SAVINGS.** Now, let's say you come into unexpected savings. For example, someone paid for your lunch or bought gas for your car etc. These could go into your short-term savings envelope. This savings envelope is for putting short-term savings that you were able to extract from cutting your expenses. Maybe someone gave you money unexpectedly for helping out. It could also go into your short-term savings. Do you have loose change? It should also go into short-term savings. Get a big jar and start emptying the loose change in your pockets into that jar. That is, whatever is left after spending the funds in the expenses envelope goes into the short-term savings envelope. The reason is because, if you don't give instructions to your money it would end up in "another person's pocket" through unplanned spending. I have put a diagram below on how you could save $1,000 in 52 weeks courtesy of Mediumsizedfamily.com

Action Item.

1. I need to develop a budget if I don't have one.

2. I need to have long-term and short-term savings.

3. I need to cut my expenses.

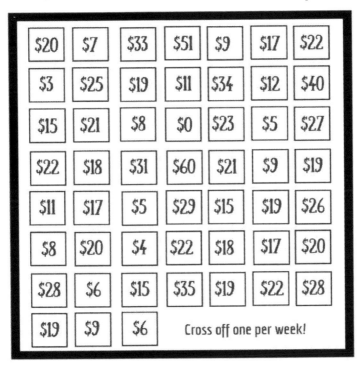

Figure 2. Money Saving Chart.[5]

CHAPTER 6

LAW OF WITHHOLDING

"...And there is one who withholds more than is right, But it leads to poverty." Prov. 11:24.

O ne night, as we finished prayer meeting, I was engaged in a conversation with an older committed lady in our church. She was coordinating some donation efforts for someone, and she blurted out something. She said, why is it that we, believers that are dedicated to serving the Lord diligently are the ones always in financial difficulties and lacking money? She said it was true in her situation.

I didn't reply, but it really bothered me. I began to talk to the Lord in my heart and asked the reason. I also asked the Holy Spirit to reveal to me what her condition was and the source. I am glad the Lord did that night, and I subsequently called her to share with her and to counsel her. After addressing the specifics of her situation, I shared with her the Law of Withholding, which I will address here.

One important financial law the Lord taught me is the law of withholding. As believers, we seem to have mastered the concept, principles and laws of giving or sowing and reaping. However, one principle or law that I see that many who excel in the law of giving haven't mastered, which sabotages the plan of God for their lives is the law of withholding.

In order to be financially successful or gain financial freedom, you must be able to master and balance the law of withholding with the law or principle of giving especially during the pandemic and even beyond. Do not forget that the principles and laws regarding money were put in place by God. Whoever doesn't follow it or flout it would suffer the consequences no matter how spirit-filled they may be.

In fact, the bible in Proverbs 11:24 mentions withholding. That verse balances giving and withholding. Notice it says the person that withholds more than is necessary or right. That means you are not expected to give everything all the time. You are expected to withhold at some point. I may get in trouble with some folks now by the next statement. It's not all the time that you are expected to give sacrificially. It's not on each occasion that you are expected to give with pain. There are some times that I had pledged a certain amount in a gathering. Then when I was in another, I didn't because I knew God would not want me to be under pressure to give.

Have you wondered why God only made 10% (at least floor level) mandatory and not more? It has to do with the law of withholding. God wants you to have enough not only to pay bills but to save and invest in other ventures that would yield more abundance. Then from that abundance of profit, you would be able to give another 10%. You must be able to have seeds to sow into business ventures or other profit yielding undertakings.

The relationship between withholding and giving could be likened to the relationship between the brake and the accelerator (gas) pedals in an automobile. In order to drive safely and arrive at one's destination, especially in one piece, you need to engage both at different times. If your feet are permanently on the accelerator, the chances are that even though you may be off to a fast start, you would soon crash and won't arrive at your destination. It could even lead to loss of life. That is what operating only on the law of giving financially would do. You would eventually run out and end up in poverty.

Likewise, if your feet is permanently on the brake, there would be no movement or progress. For this analogy, it means refusing to give and only operating on the law or principle of withholding. This would also end in poverty as you would not make any appreciable progress. Besides, you won't receive the blessings that accompany giving. Just like the brake and accelerator complement each other to safely arrive at the desired destination, also, the laws of giving and withholding need to operate collaboratively to achieve financial independence.

Do you know that God has not called you to be the Elshaddai meeting everyone's needs? No. That job is only for Him alone. You have limited resources. Only God is unlimited. Let God be God, and you remain you. If you don't learn how to balance and operate the law of withholding, you may not have anything to give anymore.

Action Item.

1. I need to review my giving patterns wherever I think I am the only solution.

2. I should not feel guilty when I have to withhold because I have not been called to meet every need.

3. If I am always withholding, I need to start giving.

CHAPTER 7

LAW OF RECEIVING

> "...Don't hesitate to accept hospitality, because those who work deserve their pay..." Luke 10:7.

Another financial law that you must understand and master as a Christian is the law of receiving. Many Christians are givers, but they find it difficult to receive. Sometimes pride gets in our way of accessing needed help. We believe we are beyond that level. I was once in that category. I always helped everyone and gave but didn't accept when I was given to. But I changed when Jesus taught me this important law, which I am sharing with you.

The bible tells us in Acts 20:35 that *"It is more blessed to give than to receive."* He did not say we should not receive. You should understand that on the way to becoming rich, Jesus would position some situations where you would be blessed along the way. It would not be the big riches you are looking for yet. Take it and give thanks. Our Lord Jesus, the Son of God, also received all through His ministry. At some point He was hosted by His friends Mary, Martha and Lazarus.

Have you ever received a large financial blessing beyond what you thought of? How did you feel? Don't feel guilty about it. Don't feel unworthy. There are some folks who would want you to apologize or feel bad for your blessings. Don't!

Eventually, you would get into a situation when your financial situation would improve greatly as you are following these laws. You may go from having one car to three cars. Does that mean you should feel guilty and give one to a friend who has none? Not necessarily. At a point, a woman broke a perfume worth a year's wages and lavished it on Jesus. He did not feel unworthy. He received it and commended the woman even when a disciple said it should have been sold and given to the poor.

Never apologize for your success. We are not called to take God's place of supplying everyone's needs. He may use us or someone else. We don't have an unlimited supply. Only God does. Don't feel pressured to turn down the blessings of God because others around you are poor except when directed by God. *I Timothy 6:17.* "*Teach those who are rich in this world...their trust should be in God, who richly gives us all we need for our enjoyment.*"

Action Item.

1. I need to learn the art of receiving no matter how small.

2. Receiving shows that I am humble enough to accept help.

3. I should not feel guilty for being blessed more than others.

CHAPTER 8

LAW OF MENTORSHIP

> *"Plans go wrong for lack of advice; many advisers bring success."* *Prov. 15:22.*

I am yet to come across anyone who succeeded financially who was not mentored. But, I have met many people who have failed financially because of a lack of mentorship. Some people balked at mentorship because they believed they have no time. Others think they could just strike out on their own and succeed. The odds of this happening are very small to nothing.

Billionaire investor Bill Ackman regularly talks about how he devoured every material he could read about Warren Buffett so that he could compress his journey to riches. Warren Buffett who is regarded as the world's most successful investor has this to say regarding mentorship. In one of his numerous speeches, he said, "think about the person whose qualities you most admire, adopt those qualities." He said if you do that, your chances of success goes up enormously.

The late Kobe Bryant was always labeled the next Michael

Jordan of basketball because of the way he played. He mimicked Jordan in play and work ethic. Jordan said he always calls him and asking questions. He even imitated Jordan to the extent that he also sticks out his tongue when he plays, which Jordan is famous for. No wonder he won five championship rings and won the most valuable player title in addition to other titles.

In Philippians 4:9, the apostle Paul said it clearly. " *Keep putting into practice all you learned and received from me - everything you heard from me and saw me doing. Then the God of peace will be with you."* Mentorship, as you know, has no regard to age but grace. The grace on a mentor is what you should look for.

When I was to break into e-commerce, I looked for mentors and paid thousands of dollars to learn from them. All of them were younger than I was. As young as I am, there are several of them that I was old enough to be their father. I put all those things aside and learned and practiced what I saw them do. That is the reason with God's help that I am able to be successful in the e-commerce sector. Without this, I would not be.

If you are serious about being a rich Christian, you must look for a mentor who is rich so that you can compress your journey to riches. There are very serious reasons why you should do this. First, you do not have all the time in the world to keep making mistakes and correcting them. A mentor already made those mistakes and could help you navigate the landmines. Secondly, you may give up without someone alongside you to assure you that it is possible.

A good mentor is very busy and would be in high demand. So, how do you get a good but hard to reach mentor's attention? One thing you could do is to help them achieve what they needed most. It could be an area where you have the expertise that the mentor doesn't. When I wanted to get into commercial real estate, especially with apartments, I reached out to a mentor who also wanted to get into billboards, and we exchanged ideas. He gave me pointers on real estate, and I put him through regarding setting up a billboard business.

Now, it's possible that sometimes you may not be able to meet with a mentor physically. It could be over the phone, a course, video call, etc. I recommend doing whatever you can to communicate with them.

Looking back now, my decision to invest in a mentor for e-commerce was well worth it. With the pandemic that overtook the world, e-commerce was one of the few sectors that experienced exponential growth.

Action Item.

1. I need to find a financial mentor to mentor me.

2. I need to think of how I could also be of value to a mentor.

PART II:
MINDSET LAWS

I n this part, we will discuss how to establish a mindset that enables an individual to become rich. The bible tells us to have the mind of Christ. I will show you some practical laws from the bible that the secular world currently uses to produce riches, which you can also use to produce wealth.

Chapter 9

Law of Meditation

"One evening as he was walking and meditating in the fields..." Genesis. 24:63.

---

ecause of how many people in the New Age movement have hijacked this, this law is one which most Christians shy away from. They can meditate on the word of God, the bible but not so much on other things such as wealth.

Ray Dialio is a billionaire who is regarded as the most successful hedge fund manager of all time. He runs a $160 billion hedge fund. He said the number one secret to his success is transcendental meditation. Again, let me reiterate. I do not practice nor believe in transcendental meditation. I don't know much about it to recommend it. The point I am driving at is that the practice of meditation is biblical. We are commanded in Joshua 1:8 to meditate on the word of God day and night.

Beyond this, I have found the practice of meditation generally to be where I receive instructions from God, gain insight into a problem, test and craft solutions. We live in an information-overloaded world that we barely have time to digest the information we have received before consuming more. We are always reacting instead of being proactive. The practice of regular meditation allows us to be proactive than reactive.

The art of regular meditation also allows us to see the big picture when done scripturally. It is all about God and His purpose. We were told that one of the practices that Isaac does was meditating. *Gen. 24:63 "One evening as he was walking and meditating in the fields..."* It is not a surprise that it yielded positive results in Chapter 26. It takes reflective meditation to hear the prompting of God on where to go and what to do during famine.

The law of meditation allows you to access knowledge and perspective beyond yours. You communicate with the Father of spirits (Hebrew 12:9) to communicate to your spirit. Don't forget that you are a spirit; you have a soul and live in a body. Because spiritists, mediums and psychics have hijacked this with demonic bent doesn't mean that the godly practice of this is wrong.

How could you engage this to profit from it? Turn off your phone and television. Have a notepad with a pen by your side to take instructions from God as He drops them in your spirit. Lay down or sit and start meditating on possibilities of your financial goals through God. Work out the details. Listen to the Holy Spirit as He whispers ideas and solutions to you in a noisy world. If that doesn't work for you, I have heard from some people that their meditation spot is while doing laundry, doing the dishes or running on the treadmill. Do whatever works for you.

Action Item.

1. I need to incorporate meditation into my daily routine.

2. I must set aside time to digest information that I have received before consuming more.

CHAPTER 10

LAW OF ADAPTATION

"Select only strong, healthy, and good-looking young men,"
he said. "Make sure they are well versed in every branch
of learning, are gifted with knowledge and good judgment,
and are suited to serve in the royal palace. Train these
young men in the language and literature of Babylon…
They were to be trained for three years, and then they
would enter the royal service."Daniel 1:4-5.

Another financial law you must observe especially if you live abroad, relocated to a new city, started a new job or found yourself in a new environment, is that of adaption. To succeed in any foreign land, you must drop your method of thinking, culture, and be trained and retrained in the country you are in, or you'd never rise to the top. You must be ready to flow in the economic wave of the country and not against it.

Daniel, Mishael (Meshach), Hananiah (Shadrach) and Azariah (Abednego), were young men taken to Babylon as slaves but rose to the top politically and financially. How could slaves within three years be one of the decision-makers in a foreign land, a foreign environment ahead of the native borns? If you say, the hand of the

Lord was upon them, that is correct but not the full story.

The Bible said they immersed themselves in the culture, language, literature and operations of Babylon for three years. It shouldn't be a surprise then that they were able to rise to the top.

If you want to be financially successful upon getting into a new environment, Jesus told me that you need to embrace the law of adaptation. If you are in a country or state foreign to yours, you need to be trained in the culture, language, and the way of life of the environment. It is impossible to import wholesale the culture and the way of life from one's own country into a foreign land and expect to be a person of influence, or operate at a higher level in the adopted country.

For example, despite the training that Daniel and his friends had in Judah, they went through retraining in Babylon. Now, adaptation for a Christian does not mean participating in ungodly practices of your new environment. It's the opposite. Daniel and his friends, in fact, refused to compromise with the sinful lifestyle of their adopted country in eating unacceptable food. While training and adapting to the culture of an adopted country or environment is required for success, you must make a distinction that the culture must be godly. A Christian should determine not to be influenced or compromise their faith in Christ.

Ungodly practices, no matter how legal and normal, must be shunned even at the risk of penalty. That was what Daniel, Azariah, Mishael, Hananiah did in rejecting the sinful gourmet food presented to them in Babylon at the risk of their lives. However, after sticking out their necks for God, He made them much better than their colleagues. He loaded them with gifts that made them unrivaled and ten times better than their colleagues in training. This vaulted them to the highest level of influence in a foreign land. That is a blueprint you can also follow today.

Many Christians have prayed to God about having an economic voice and political say so in their countries, states and even local governments, but God has not answered their prayers. One of the reasons is because they have not been trained in the protocols of where they longed to be. Before King David was taken to the palace to become king, even though he was anointed as one, he had to learn palace protocols while he was with King Saul. This firsthand up-close look allowed him to escape the mistakes of Saul.

America is filled with stories of immigrants who came to the U.S., trained and immersed themselves in the culture, and succeeded. Not many people knew that one of the founders of Google, Sergey Brin, who is also one of the richest persons on the planet, was not born in the U.S. He was born in Moscow in the former Soviet Union. He immigrated along with his parents to the U.S. He attended elementary, high school, and college in Maryland before heading to Stanford. He made friends at Stanford, especially with Larry Page and others with whom they found Google.

Do you also know Jerry Yang, the founder of Yahoo, who is currently worth $2.3 billion, only knew the English word "shoe" when he immigrated to America from Taiwan? Despite this, he also applied the financial law of adaptation. He was trained. He went to Stanford and excelled.[6]

To succeed in America now, or as an immigrant in any other country this is not an option. If you don't have close friends in the new environment you are in, you have not adapted. Adaptation is a must to rise to the top and become rich in a new environment.

Action Item.

1. Have I adapted to my new environment or expect it to adapt to me?

2. Do I have any close friends in my new environment?

43

3. Do others in my new environment easily get along with me?

4. Can I be recommended to others in my new environment?

CHAPTER 11

LAW OF DELAYED GRATIFICATION

*"You must have the same attitude that Christ Jesus had...
he gave up his divine privileges... When he appeared in
human form, he humbled himself in obedience to God...
Therefore, God elevated him to the place of highest honor
and gave him the name above all other names." Philippians
2:5,7,8,9.*

For the most part, if you are just starting out, it is not possible to live in comfort and luxury and build a successful business at the same time. Something has to give. You either build a successful business, or you live in comfort and pay for it later. I learned something called opportunity cost in high school. There is a cost to every opportunity. You'd have to forgo one thing for another.

I have read and listened to the story of several successful people who followed this principle. Tyler Perry (Film Producer), Steve Harvey (Media Personality), J.K. Rowling (Harry Potter), Robert Kiyosaki (Rich Dad, Poor Dad) all at one point lived out of their cars and while at the same time, were working on their businesses.

They planned and worked their businesses when there wasn't a roof over their heads save that of their automobile. They tended their businesses, and afterward they were able to afford a life of comfort.

Do you know that our Lord Jesus modeled the example of delayed gratification? The bible mentioned that because of the reward set before Him, He endured the cross. He became human. What was the reward? After He had gone to the cross, the Father would exalt Him to the highest position and give Him a name that is above every other name. Everything in the world has a name. Now the Father was going to give Him a name that would be the Supreme above all names.

As you must have known, divinity humbling Himself to become humanity is demeaning. Then suffering abuse, shame, beating from the hands of those you could easily wipe out is also hard to stomach. In addition, the bible called His death on the cross a criminal's death *(Phil 2:8)*. But it was all for one purpose. It was to earn that reward. The reward of high exaltation and the name above all names.

To become rich as a Christian, you must have the same attitude as Jesus and delay your gratification. *"You must have the same attitude that Christ Jesus had...he gave up his divine privileges..."* You would need to give up some comfort and luxury. While I'm not recommending that you should live out of your car, especially if you are married with children, but you could put that plan to purchase a house on hold. Remain in your apartment so you could free up the resources to "tend your field and afterward build your house." If you already own a home, think about remaining in the home or downsize if you have to. Luxury and comfort can afford to wait, becoming financially independent, and building a successful business cannot afford to. *"Hard choices, easy life. Easy choices, hard life."* Says Jerzey Gregorek.

If you do fail to build your business before your house, by this I mean put in the hard work and live frugally before comfort, you'd be paying for your comfort through your wage income or the sweat of your brow. The better way is to live in comfort paid for by a business that you own.

I have a close friend who I saw put this in practice. He had always desired to buy a BMW 7 series. He said he wasn't going to pay for it. Someone else would. He had businesses. From the income he generated from the business he was able to by the BMW. He didn't have to sweat for it. His business solved someone's problem who indirectly paid for it.

So, delay your gratification for that shiny Mercedes and the massive mansion. Instead put your sweat into building a successful business to earn a living and afterwards buy the Mercedes or build that mansion.

Action Item.

1. I need to master the law of delaying gratification.

2. I need to stay away from those who are unable to delay gratification.

3. I need to prioritize my goals.

4. I need to develop a means to reward myself.

CHAPTER 12

LAW OF PAYING FOR VALUE

"Buy truth—don't sell it for love or money; buy wisdom,
buy education, buy insight." Proverbs 23:23. MSG.

I see something grossly anti-law of prosperity. It is individuals wanting to get stuff for free. I do believe in financial prudence. Sound financial management is a requirement for becoming rich. However, it is not possible to leech your way to enduring financial riches. You must pay for value.

In the principal scripture above, it mentioned paying for truth, wisdom, education, insight, and says don't sell them. They are values. That means in any business that you may want to get into, there is a truth. There is an insight.

Beyond the knowledge that is required in any venture, you also need the wisdom and insight of those who had excelled in that field. How they applied the knowledge. This wisdom, education, insight could come from buying their books, paying for their courses, etc.

You see, God has designed life in a way that everyone that has or provides value must be rewarded. Anyone who has value that is serving humanity must be rewarded. For example, the accountant who does your taxes needs to be compensated for their time. They, in turn, would need to pay maybe the person that tutors their son or daughter, or the company where they buy their accounting software from. These are obvious examples that people know. However, when it comes to areas such as financial advice, consulting, many do not want to pay. They would be looking for a method to get it for free. There is something that paying for value does to you. Beyond meeting your immediate need, for those who are Christians, there is a grace (good fortune for non-Christians) on the person providing the value that you attract to your life.

Anyone who is successful financially or otherwise, carries an intangible grace that makes it possible. This is what you see sometimes when some people pay authors more than the value of a book. They are not only buying the book, but they also want the grace that enables the author to attain that success to come upon them as well.

Don't forget that becoming rich or financially independent has a lot to do with making behavioral changes. Rich people pay for value wherever they find it.

One of the wealthiest men in the world, regarded as the most successful investor is Warren Buffett. Buffett does an annual charity lunch every year. This is where individuals from around the world bid for the opportunity to have lunch with him, bringing seven friends and asking any question that they want. The winning bid for 2020, at the time of this writing was $4.6 million. If you are broke or poor reading this, your natural reaction would be this is too much. Undeniably, those that bid believe there is a value that having lunch with him brings that is why they are willing to pay for it. In 2010, Ted Weschler won the bid with $2,626,311. He won again in 2011, paying $2,626,411. Weschler said he discovered Buffett's investing approach while studying at the University of Pennsylvania's Wharton School of Business. He had also been applying this investment approach.

According to him, "From then on, I kept my eye open for anything that had to do with [Buffett]. It was on my list that at some point, I wanted to meet the guy."[7] Weschler currently works for Buffett and is rumored to be his company's future Chief Investment Officer.

To be financially independent in the pandemic and beyond, pay for value. Sometimes what you pay for value is not in cash. It could be in kind. To pay in kind, it has to be what the person needs. For example, there was a story in the bible of a woman with an alabaster jar of expensive perfume (Luke 7:36-50). She recognized the value of Jesus and spared no expense to show it. She anointed the feet of Jesus with a year's salary worth of oil. What she did was significant for Jesus. She was forgiven as a result.

Action Item.

1. I need to develop the habit of appreciating and paying for value.

2. Is there anyone that I admire that I need to appreciate?

CHAPTER 13

LAW OF EXCEPTIONS

> *"Nevertheless, lest we offend them, go to the sea, cast in a hook, and take the fish that comes up first. And when you have opened its mouth, you will find a piece of money; take that and give it to them for Me and you." Matt. 17:27.*

During COVID-19 and beyond, two things that would probably be in the prayer list of many Christians would be miraculous provision of money and supernatural debt cancellation. I believe that I need to discuss this law because many believers have been affected by this and do not understand the ways of God on money.

Financial law of exceptions involves meeting money obligations outside the established financial principles. It could be what is called miraculous provision of money or debt cancellation that defies the norm. For example, when Jesus told Peter to go and fish, and he caught money from the mouth of the fish to pay their taxes that is an exception and not the norm.

Exceptions, as it connotes, is not the rule. Many Christians expect that their financial independence would come from the financial law of exception. The fact is that the majority would not benefit from this. God does this as He sees fit. I would address this from multiple angles for a proper understanding of what I mean.

Miracle Money

First, I want you to know that I believe in financial exceptions and God providing miracle money. I know firsthand, people who have experienced this, including in our congregation. For example, a sister testified to finding over $11,000 in a bag they had without having put any money in the bag. It was an amount needed that met their needs. On another occasion, a lady again testified in our church of miraculous supply. In fact, she was screaming on the phone. She needed some money to pay some bills. She checked her account and found thousands of dollars there. She tried to trace the deposit, which was made in another state, and the name of the depositor says, "Jesus Christ." These are true stories. I know the people involved firsthand. If you are not bored, I would give you one more. My Pastor needed some money at some point. The Lord had already told him to always ask him when he is in need of money. This time he did. The Lord instructed him to look into his jacket, and he did as instructed by God and found over $1,000 there.

All these are exceptions in financial laws for Christians. I do not recollect ever having gotten miracle money myself though I believe in it. You should also believe God that it is possible to have a miracle money moment but don't build your financial future around it. A lot of times, God looks at your capacity or capability per time before doing this.

Miracle Debt Cancelation.

Another financial exception is miracle debt cancellations. I am yet to meet a Christian who doesn't want a miracle debt cancellation. I believe in it as well. I have seen God do it in the lives of many people. One of my brothers had over $76,000 in debt miraculously canceled. I still believe God can do this in my life as well. I don't rule God out of anything. However, the truth is that the majority of Christians would probably not experience miraculous debt cancellation. It is usually an exception. For example, if the Lord wants to teach you to be financially prudent, you may not have miraculous debt cancellation. No matter how much you fast, pray and yes - sow. It may not happen.

Learn to identify how God wants to solve your debt situation. Regardless of what you believe would happen, sound financial practices are always approved by God. His word says in *Psalm 37:21, The wicked borrow and never repay, but the godly are generous givers.* Accordingly, it is better to put in place a financial plan to pay off your debts.

Comparison

Another dimension of the law of exceptions that you should be aware of is regarding comparing yourself to others with their financial journey. There would be some folks you know around you that do not stress for money. They don't have to struggle or pound the hard pavement as much as you do before they get results. It appears that everything they touch turns to profit. When you ask them how they made it, you may discover that they are not doing anything extraordinary to be financially wealthy. In fact, you have done more than they did, but your results are not comparable. They are exceptions.

You cannot build your financial life around those exceptions as well. You must be able to quickly identify those with exceptions. You can learn from them what you may have in common but exercise caution in building your financial path around their experiences. For example, Warren Buffett is one of the richest people on the planet.

He is worth an estimated $86 billion. One of the things that helped him was that he said he knew at the age of 11, exactly what he wanted to be when he grew up and followed through. This is what he is doing today. Except for sport athletes and a few others, not many know what they would become in life at age 11.

Also, observe King David in the bible and his son Solomon. David fought many wars for many years before he could be established, attain wealth and have peace years later. But Solomon did not fight any war. He started with peace. If both were to give you advice on financial independence, they would probably give from different perspectives based on their experiences on their path to fulfillment.

Does this mean the law of financial exception is useless to you? No. As I discussed earlier, don't rule out God's ability to invade your finances with miracle money or miraculous debt cancelations. Still, don't build your life around them. Exercise sound financial discipline in addition to this. Also, regarding comparison, you can benefit by identifying a wealthy individual who started with challenges similar to yours. You'd have more in common. Chances are what worked for them would be a tool for you to use.

Action Item.

1. I must recognize and understand the law of exceptions.

2. I must know that God may choose not to bless me via exceptions.

3. I should visit https://www.daveramsey.com/get-started/debt for some debt resources.

4. I need to identify wealthy individuals who started with challenges similar to mine and learn from them.

PART III:
STEWARDSHIP LAWS

Since we are stewards of God's riches, which are entrusted into our care, we will discuss different ways we can demonstrate this stewardship. When you effectively obey these laws of stewardship, He guarantees it would trigger riches in many ways beyond our capacity to contain them. I show the many ways with real-life examples to trigger them into your life.

CHAPTER 14

LAW OF GOD FIRST

"Honor God with everything you own; give him the first and the best. Your barns will burst, your wine vats will brim over." Proverbs 3:9. MSG.

I f you want to be rich in God's way, you must put God first. God must trump every other need in your life. This includes your mortgage and any other bills. Don't worry; God would not allow you to be put to shame.

This is one of the tests you would face from time to time. Putting God first is the greatest demonstration of your faith in the God you profess you believe in. Until you pass the test of faithfulness, especially in tough times, God doesn't believe or reckon that you fear Him. We saw this when God tested Abraham to sacrifice his only son Isaac. *Genesis 22:12 "Don't lay a hand on the boy!" the angel said. "Do not hurt him in any way, for now I know that you truly fear God. You have not withheld from me even your son, your only son."*

I have so many practical examples of Jesus drilling this to me until I lost the fear that I would ever be financially stranded. I remembered prior to losing my first house, I had just gotten some money, which would have helped with our mortgage, but I instead paid my tithe. I still lost the house. It was a very painful experience, but God always had a better plan. I went through many other tests with God before He began to trust me with more financial resources. When you put God first, you give Him access to meet your needs according to His riches and not according to your human limitations.

Do you remember the story of Hannah, the mother of Prophet Samuel in the Bible? It is found in the book of First Samuel 1. It shows that when we put God first, we give Him a deal He can't refuse.

Many Christians don't know that they could give God a deal He could never refuse! All Hannah's years of barrenness ended when she decided to give God a deal He couldn't turn down. She prayed violently about her condition, specifically turning all the provocations to her advantage. The deal-breaker, however, came when her request aligned with God's purpose. God was looking for a prophet, and she gave God a deal He could never refuse. A prophet! She said if God gives her a male child, that child would be given back to God to serve Him all the days of his life. To compensate her, God gave her five more children.

So, do you want to be rich? You may try giving God a deal He can't refuse! Put Him first in all you do, especially in your finances. When you put God first in your finances, it shows that money doesn't have a hold on you. You have a hold on money. Money is not your master. It is your servant, which is where it should be.

"But remember the LORD your God, for it is he who gives you the ability to produce wealth, and so confirms his covenant, which he swore to your ancestors, as it is today." Deuteronomy 8:18.

Wealth, riches or financial independence gained without God as the sole focus would often lead to emptiness, depression, sorrow or even suicide. The way life is designed is for God to be the reason, the center, the beginning, the middle, the end of all. A proper understanding of this would give you the right perspective in the pursuit of financial success. Absence of this would make you miserable. I have discovered that riches gained aside from God only goes to satisfy wants. Because wants is not the reason man was created, they often leave us empty.

I remember sadly the story of a young man that I often studied and look up to for mentorship in e-commerce. At the age of 19, he already became a millionaire. He was doing revenues close to a million dollars a month. Because of his access to such unimaginable wealth, he was able to afford luxury cars such as Lamborghini, which he paid for with cash. However, each time I see his video on YouTube, I began to perceive in my spirit that something was off. While this may not be apparent to everyone, to me, it appears that he was trying to overcompensate for something. A few months later we heard that he died. Put God first.

Action Item

1. Evaluate my life and see where I am not putting God first.

2. Make a change to put God first.

3. Give God a deal He can't refuse.

Chapter 15

Law of Tithing the First Part of Income

A tithe is the first 10% of your gross income or earnings, and any other money that is given to you that goes to God. A Christian should set this aside to God first. There have been several controversies surrounding this. But the bible says, *"Bring all the tithes into the storehouse so there will be enough food in my Temple. If you do," says the Lord of Heaven's Armies, "I will open the windows of heaven for you. I will pour out a blessing so great you won't have enough room to take it in! Try it! Put me to the test!"* Malachi 3:10. Many have said it was only applicable under the law. This is not so.

The principle of God requiring a portion of whatever He gives us predates even Moses or Abraham. It started at the Garden of Eden. God told Adam and Eve that they could eat from any tree in the garden except one - the Tree of Good and Evil (Gen. 2:16-17). That was the tithe. It was God's portion. You may ask how? In Gen. 3:22, after they ate the fruit, it says, *"Then the LORD God said, "Look, the human beings have become like us..".* God's portion is non-negotiable. He drove them out of the garden.

Are you familiar with Abraham? Yeah? That guy that was a friend of God? The one who was greatly blessed and became our example of faith in God? He paid tithes before the law of Moses. *Gen. 14:20. "and blessed be God Most High, who has delivered your enemies into your hand." Then Abram gave Melchizedek a tenth of everything."*

The blessings of every Christian flows from Abraham as written in:

Galatians 3:8-9 & 29 "...God proclaimed this good news to Abraham long ago when he said, "All nations will be blessed through you." So all who put their faith in Christ share the same blessing Abraham received because of his faith. And now that you belong to Christ, you are the true children of Abraham. You are his heirs, and God's promise to Abraham belongs to you."

Many Christians today claim the blessings of Abraham but do not engage in the practices required by God to invoke the blessings. That could be the reason why you are not experiencing Abraham's level of blessings. Notice that Abraham gave the TITHES OF ALL! We are required to pay a tenth of all income that we earn and or money given to us. Abraham tithed (Gen. 14:20.), Isaac tithed, Jacob tithed *("... I will present to God a tenth of everything he gives me," Gen 28:22.)*

The Lord Jesus Christ has this to say on tithing when rebuking the Pharisees for their hypocrisies. *"What sorrow awaits you teachers of religious law and you Pharisees. Hypocrites! For you are careful to tithe even the tiniest income from your herb gardens, but you ignore the more important aspects of the law—justice, mercy, and faith.* **You should tithe, yes,** *but do not neglect the more important things." Matthew 23:23.*

Personally, I have paid tithes faithfully for decades. Granted, it could be difficult to start or to do. Your entire, complete income may not be enough to meet your bills even without deducting tithes. Paying tithes may put further strain on your finances in the initial stages. That was my experience, but that is the nature of obeying God despite the difficulty of your situations. God would always reward obedience that would cost you.

I mentioned that I had paid tithes, even in extreme circumstances. What I was telling God by those actions was that I trust Him to take care of me regardless of what I see. I have seen the rewards of giving tithes to God. I have also seen practical modern-day examples where God withheld blessings from believers and asked them to pay tithes first.

I remembered the case of a brother who once came to me for prayers. Many things were not working for him. One of them was that he had problems with passing his driving test, which was required for the job he wanted. He had taken it more than three times with no success. When he came to me, the first thing the Lord to me to ask him was whether he was paying his tithes faithfully. I did, and he said no. I then explained to him that to get God involved in his situation, he cannot be violating his law. This would give the devil the legal ground to successfully accuse him before God. Don't forget that the Bible says Satan is the accuser of God's people ("For the accuser of our brothers and sisters...the one who accuses them before our God day and night. Rev. 12:10). The brother said he would make the changes, so I prayed for him. He came back and told me that he has started paying his tithes. He went back, took the driving test, and passed. There are other stories that I could tell as well.

Do you agree as a Christian, all that you are and have belongs to God? Then you should keep in mind that tithing is just the floor level as far as God is concerned. There are times that God would require you to give more than your tithes. I will give some of my examples when I talk about the law of Sacrifice and Giving to Servants of God.

65

We often read stories in the Bible that excites us because of the happy ending but we forget to take into account the painful cost of in the process of putting God first. An example is the story of how God exalted Daniel to highest positions, but we forget that he went to the lions' den obeying God to get there. If you cannot pay your tithes to God, it may be difficult to go into the lion's den for your faith. Whatever you cannot release to God is your master. It has taken God's position in that area of your life. Release it to God and let Him be the Lord of all.

Action Item.

1. Review my finances, whether I am paying tithes correctly and faithfully.

2. Ask God for forgiveness and promise to start paying my tithes correctly and faithfully.

3. Boldly ask God to open the windows of heaven and pour out a blessing that I have no room to contain.

CHAPTER 16

LAW OF GIVING TO YOUR PARENTS

*"In this way, you let them disregard their needy parents.
And so you cancel the word of God in order to hand down
your own tradition..." Mark 7:12-13.*

Another form of giving that the Lord expects is giving to one's parents. It is required by the Lord as a way to honor and take care of them. It is part of their earthly reward. If your parents are still living, you are obligated to give to them. They are investors in your life, and God expects every investor to be rewarded. Rewarding investors is a sure way to financial independence.

God has given parents a certain level of authority that whatever they say about the future of their children happens. If they curse their child, that child would be cursed. If they bless their child, that child would be blessed. Have you abandoned your parents, or not on speaking terms with them because of something that they did which hurt you? I plead with you that for the sake of Christ, you should forgive them.

There is a story in the bible you might have read before in Genesis 35:22. Reuben, who was the firstborn of Jacob, slept with one of his step-mothers, Bilhah, who was one of Jacob's wives. Jacob did not make a mention of it until on his death bed, where he cursed him. In *Genesis 49:3-4.* "*Reuben, you are my firstborn, my strength, the child of my vigorous youth. You are first in rank and first in power. But you are as unruly as a flood, and you will be first no longer. For you went to bed with my wife; you defiled my marriage couch.*" Then Jacob transferred the double portion blessings that were to be on Reuben and gave it to Joseph.

Next, Jacob took it even further. He elevated Joseph's sons, Manasseh and Ephraim, to be on the same level as separate tribes of Israel, just like their other uncles like Reuben, Judah, etc. It permanently altered the tribes of Israel forever. This is Jacob speaking here. *Genesis. 48:5* "*Now I am claiming as my own sons these two boys of yours, Ephraim and Manasseh, who were born here in the land of Egypt before I arrived. They will be my sons, just as Reuben and Simeon are.*"

Now, how did Jacob patriarch secure the generational blessing from Isaac their dad? It was when he gave to him. He gave Isaac venison that he loves. This triggered the generational blessings to flow to Jacob and not Esau (Gen. 27:27-29).

Still not convinced? This verse shows just how powerful the authority God has given parents is. It can even invalidate vows. *Numbers 30:3-5.* "*If a young woman makes a vow to the LORD or a pledge under oath while she is still living at her father's home, and her father hears of the vow or pledge and does not object to it, then all her vows and pledges will stand.* ___But if her father refuses to let her fulfill the vow or pledge on the day he hears of it, then all her vows and pledges will become invalid.___ *The LORD will forgive her because her father would not let her fulfill them.*

I encourage you to reach out to your parents if it's still possible, especially if they are still alive. Forgive them if they have hurt you for your peace of mind. Bless them with what you have. If they are able to bless you in return, that's great!

Action Item.

1. Reach out to my parents or parental figure and make amends.

2. Reach out to my parents or parental figure and begin to bless them financially no matter how small.

CHAPTER 17

LAW OF GIVING TO SERVANTS OF GOD

"If you receive a prophet as one who speaks for God, you will be given the same reward as a prophet." Matthew 10:41.

"Those who are taught the word of God should provide for their teachers, sharing all good things with them."Galatians 6:6.

In our present day, giving to Pastors, Priests and other ministers have gotten a bad rap. There have been abuses from some servants of God regarding their relationships with the people under their care. Many have turned their members or those seeking help from them into a sort of personal bank to fulfill their desires. As a result, it has provoked a strong backlash from within and outside the church. It has gotten to a point where most preachers are viewed as charlatans. However, as with anything God does and Satan manipulates, it does not mean that a real one doesn't exist. Prepare to give to servants of God if you want to move upward in God's blessings. Again, this is one area also where I have been instructed and tested severally by

God.

First, let me clear something up that may ruffle some feathers but is actually beneficial for you to know. We are all equal before God. Both the servants of God and the congregants are equal before God. However, we do not all have equal grace on our heads. The grace that God gives to His servants stands them out when it comes to dealing with issues on earth. Think of this grace as God's special empowerment to perform specific tasks. For example, recall when Samson was empowered as a judge in Israel in Judges 16. Even though all other Israelites like him are equal before God, yet he was the only one empowered to kill the philistines or lions with bare hands. Anyone other person who tries it would likely become a snack.

Second, in the New Testament, the Bible says this concerning the ministerial gifts, "*And He Himself gave some to be apostles, some prophets, some evangelists, and some pastors and teachers, for the equipping of the saints for the work of ministry, for the edifying of the body of Christ.*" *Ephesians 4:11-13. KJV.* Noticed that Jesus gave some, not all.

Now, let's break it down. Because of their office or roles as apostles, pastors, prophets and so forth, anyone who accepts them and gives to them, would receive in return the reward of the grace that God has put on that office that they occupy. As described in Matthew 10:42, the unseen grace that God has embedded in that office would automatically be triggered and would compensate those who give to them.

Let me share with you a secret. If there is anything that has given me a fast track in spiritual growth, in the "giftings" of God and anointing, it is giving to the servants of God. I will share some stories with you. But first, let us see what the bible says. I refer to the bible not just to validate my point, but because God is only committed to implementing His word. If I make up something that is not backed up by God, it may sound good, but there would be zero rewards if you try it.

Accordingly, let's see a story from the bible. In 2 Kings 4:8-17, we saw a story that we could learn from. It was about a wealthy married woman that's probably old but childless. She started ministering (giving) to the man of God, Elisha.

She started by first persuading him to eat food every day from her house.

She recognized and valued the man of God. Others might have seen him and just let him pass on by, but she didn't. She didn't relate to him as just another person or become too familiar with the grace that was on him.

Then, she did something that is extraordinary even by today's standard. She built a room for the man of God to rest. That is even a lot considering that the man of God was not going to be actually living there but only to pass by for a few and rest. We were not told where the man of God was going to, but she was supporting his ministry. This singular act triggered what she didn't even expect. It solved a problem of childlessness that she had battled for years. She didn't pray on this issue. Rather, honoring the man of God, who is God's representative on earth, gave her great dividend. Not to be missed is that she never even believed that it was going to happen. But then her continuous giving to Elisha already spoke ahead for her. Her seed was already a faith action. Consequently, when Elisha released the word, it was irreversible.

I believe the Lord put the above story in the Bible to let us know the importance of honoring, supporting and caring for His ministers. Even and especially when they don't request it. Elisha never requested it. We should also remember that it must have cost the woman and her family quite a huge sum to do this. Still, both the husband and wife agreed, and this turned out to be a great blessing meeting the most important need of their lives.

Again, there are several personal examples that I could share.

I remembered a few years ago, I was at a crossroads of acquiring a property. I had tried everything, and it appeared not to be working. So I said I would summon a radical faith. I would not recommend this if you have not built your faith level to that point.

I took out a loan. It was expensive. I divided it and dared the devil to resist the grace on the lives of my spiritual fathers. I went and gave it to seven of them and told them I want the reward of the grace on their lives to attend to the situation in my life. Prior to that, I had told my wife that by the following month, we would have gotten the property. We got the property after taking that action. Years prior, we were unsuccessful.

Aside from this, I regularly give to my Pastor in my church, and I have seen how God distributed the same grace of the gift of words of knowledge, prophetic and healings operating in his life on my life. I had prayed severally for those graces, but it wasn't until I continued to give for years, a practice that still continues to this day, that the Lord released the giftings into my life.

Let me add just one more. I promise, and it won't bore you. There was this time not quite long ago. The Lord told me to empty my bank account and give it to two particular ministers of His in sort of 90% to 10% ratio. I do not know the reason, but I did. It was a particularly difficult and challenging time financially for me. That year was rough and tough. I did not get any financial reward or any reward back from it, but I continued to trust God.

Surprisingly, a few years later, it unleashed another level of God's giftings in my life. The Lord started telling me specifically where to invest. He would give me specific company names and the next products they have in the pipeline. He would give me secrets of some insider deliberations. He would take me in the spirit to countries and particularly cities that I have absolutely no clue about and tell me information no one knows.

For example, I remembered sometime in 2019, I told the Lord that I needed some money for a major investment that I wanted to make. As I laid in my bed one Sunday evening, He flashed before me that I should go and buy the stocks of a company called Beyond Meat. I did. In seven days, the stock went up by over 100% from when I bought it. I was elated. I sold it within that period and had enough to fund my investment.

When you give to genuine servants of God, it automatically triggers the grace of God upon the life of that minister to manifest in your life. The reward often shows up in areas where you need the most help. If you want to breakthrough financially, you should identify a servant of God with the grace of financial prosperity and give them to them. As I mentioned before, Abraham gave to Melchizedek the Priest of God and was blessed. *"Consider then how great this Melchizedek was. Even Abraham, the great patriarch of Israel, recognized this by giving him a tenth of what he had taken in battle. "And without question, the person who has the power to give a blessing is greater than the one who is blessed."Hebrews 7:4,7.*

To support grace on a servant of God, let me share briefly with you a testimony out of many of a college student who had texted me for prayers regarding his finances. I have included both the before picture of his stock portfolio and the after picture after I texted my prayers back to him.

"Good evening sir, I just wanted to reach out to you sir to please pray for me. In a tight spot financially that I need some money by the end of the month realistically by the 25th really to sort out some bills and matters for school as I go back around then also."

Before   **After**

Figure 3. Stock Portfolio.

"*Good evening Mike. You are blessed and highly favored. I pray that the mercy of God speak for you now. May financial help arise for you where you least expect. May the Lord raise a fish with your gold coin to locate you for more than enough in Jesus name. May you have more than enough for all you need to do in Jesus name.*

Action Item

1. Check my belief system on what I believe about the servants of God.

2. I need to start regularly giving to my Pastor if I haven't.

3. I need to prayerfully ask God, which of His servants I should start giving to.

4. I need to know that I need the grace of God on my servant of God to take me to my next level.

CHAPTER 18

LAW OF SACRIFICIAL GIVING

"…No, I insist on buying it, for I will not present burnt offerings to the Lord my God that have cost me nothing…"
2 Samuel 24:24.

I t could be particularly challenging to give to money sacrificially to God during financially challenging times. This is one area that Jesus has taught and tested me and. This law may not be for everybody. It is only for you if you want to be a major blessing to others. If you want to be a major custodian of God's blessings. Think of the Federal Reserve in the U.S., the European Central Bank in Europe or the Bank of England in the U.K who are bankers to other banks. Yep. That kind of blessing. Being God's custodian in lending to nations' kind of blessing.

As you begin to walk with Jesus in your finances, when He wants to promote you to a major level of financial breakthrough or higher level of blessing or grace, He would require sacrificial giving from you. Sacrificial giving is a major requirement to that path. I dare to say that it is a law set it in stone. All through the bible, I have never come across anyone blessed by God that He did not test with someone or something near and dear to them to offer as a sacrifice.

Anyone that wants to become the "rich" that Jesus promised in 2 Corinthians 8:9 must know and prepare for a day or time that God would require sacrificial giving of financial resources they have made plans for. If that is you, there would be a parting with the dearest assets to you. You would have to let go of what is in your hands to inherit the future the Lord has for you.

I have come to the conclusion that the major blessing lies beyond our comfort zones. For example, do you remember the story of Abraham? God had promised Abraham that He would make him a blessing. He would make him a great nation, and from him, all the nations of the earth would be blessed. God had promised and guaranteed him children (Gen. 12:1-3). So it seemed sort of contradictory that God would ask him again to go and sacrifice his only son.

Some time later, God tested Abraham's faith. "Abraham!" God called. "Yes," he replied. "Here I am." "Take your son, your only son— yes, Isaac, whom you love so much—and go to the land of Moriah. Go and sacrifice him as a burnt offering on one of the mountains, which I will show you." Genesis 22:1-2

There are some basic truths this should teach us. In following God, on the way to obtaining the promise, we should be prepared to be stretched and tasked beyond our comfort zones. You should be prepared to lose it all. Anything within your comfort zone is still based on human strength and capacity, which God doesn't need to accomplish His purpose. Real and major faith needed for the major blessing doesn't kick in until we are beyond our comfort zones. It is where there is no safety net. It is either God shows up, or we perish. When you have been stretched successfully beyond your comfort zone several times, and you held on in faith, abandoning yourself totally to the hand of God to do as He pleases, fear loses its grip on you. You are no longer cowered into playing it safe. You can absolutely trust God in that area of your life.

When they arrived at the place where God had told him to go, Abraham built an altar and arranged the wood on it. Then he tied his son, Isaac, and laid him on the altar on top of the wood. And Abraham picked up the knife to kill his son as a sacrifice. At that moment the angel of the LORD called to him from heaven, "Abraham! Abraham!" "Yes," Abraham replied. "Here I am!" "Don't lay a hand on the boy!" the angel said. "Do not hurt him in any way, for now I know that you truly fear God. You have not withheld from me even your son, your only son." Genesis 22:9-12.

Because Abraham obeyed God sacrificially, God then unleashed irrevocable blessings on him.

"This is what the LORD says: Because you have obeyed me and have not withheld even your son, your only son, I swear by my own name that 17I will certainly bless you. I will multiply your descendants beyond number, like the stars in the sky and the sand on the seashore. Your descendants will conquer the cities of their enemies. And through your descendants all the nations of the earth will be blessed—all because you have obeyed me." Genesis 22:16-18.

Major blessings come on the runway of sacrificial giving. I have had several examples when the Lord told me to give sacrificially. Sometimes it is personal instructions; other times it is occasions in the church for His work.

On one occasion, there was an opportunity to give in building a new cathedral for our church because our current place was small. This was at a time that my family still had financial challenges and not a whole lot. Of course, there were debts, mortgage, student loans, credit card and other bills.

Anyway, we pledged to give three thousand dollars as a family. I had already redeemed a substantial amount of what we pledged. Then I redeemed $1,000. That night the Lord woke me up and told me to ask for anything that I wanted. He said, "Ask of Me, Ask of Me, Ask for More!" I wrote down seven major prayer requests for my life. There are so many things that I need to fulfill my purpose in life. I will be a great fool to center all my requests on money. Money is just one of them.

Meanwhile, up to date, those prayers are still being answered. I am shocked when I see God's hands every day based on that request. It is mind-boggling. If you get this opportunity, don't waste it just on asking for money. I will share more when I discuss the law of giving to the poor and preemptive giving.

Action Item.

1. I need to have a mentality that all I have belongs to God.

2. I must take steps that prove to God that money doesn't have control over me.

3. I must know that if God must trust me with great riches, He would first test me with sacrificial giving.

CHAPTER 19

LAW OF GIVING TO THE POOR, ORPHANS, LESS PRIVILEGED & AS INSPIRED

I was in the train station awaiting my ride when a homeless man approached me, asking for a dollar. I gave him twenty dollars. He was really excited and began to thank me. He had sat down next to me. Usually, when I give money like that, I tell the person that it's because of Jesus and then start engaging them asking if they know Him.

Prior to meeting the man, I had withdrawn a little over a hundred dollars on my way before boarding the train. As we continued to talk, the Lord told me to empty all that is in my wallet and give it to him. I needed the money, but I obeyed. The man was crying and thanking me. He could not believe his eyes! Again, I told him it was Jesus. The following week the Lord gave me $6,000. There are several instances of these sorts of occurrences that I have lost count, and

God had been amazing to me.

Many people use their lenses to judge everyone that approaches them for money and because of their principle never give anything to them. I would encourage you not to do so. But instead, allow your heart to be open to God's leading. Sometimes, angels would appear as homeless men to bless you, and you would miss your blessings.

We must remember that we are expected to do good deeds with our financial resources. God expects us as His children to mimic His character by giving to the poor, needy and less privileged among us, as we are inspired.

Don't forget that the principal requirement for receiving forgiveness from God is that we must first give it to others. God longs for people that would take care of the poor, orphans, and the less privileged for Him. He is so particular about it that He called giving to the poor lending to Him. Would you like to lend God some money today? Give to the less privileged.

Action Item.

1. I need to identify the poor, orphans and the less privileged and extend financial blessings to them.

CHAPTER 20

LAW OF PREEMPTIVE GIVING

"the king summoned Nathan the prophet. "Look," David said, "I am living in a beautiful cedar palace, but the Ark of God is out there in a tent!" Nathan replied to the king, "Go ahead and do whatever you have in mind, for the Lord is with you." 2 Samuel 7:2-3.

One of the financial laws of becoming rich that I have tested and that works is preemptive giving. It works both for God and for fellow human beings. Preemptive giving is when you give something you perceived that someone needs without the individual expressly asking for it.

King David had this idea to build a temple for God. God never asked him to. Nonetheless, he observed that the Ark of Covenant and every other sacred item for God's worship was housed in a tent. Then he made up his mind to build a befitting temple for God. *2 Samuel 7:2"...See now, I dwell in a house of cedar, but the ark of God dwells inside tent curtains."*

As you know, David ended up not building the temple because the Lord gave the task to his son. He did make the materials available, nonetheless. Yet, because of that act to build a temple for God, it provoked God to make an everlasting covenant with David. He released more unimaginable blessings to his generations forever. Here are some of what God said.

"...And I will give you rest from all your enemies. "'Furthermore, the Lord declares that he will make a house for you—a dynasty of kings! For when you die and are buried with your ancestors, I will raise up one of your descendants, your own offspring, and I will make his kingdom strong. He is the one who will build a house—a temple— for my name. And I will secure his royal throne forever. I will be his father, and he will be my son. If he sins, I will correct and discipline him with the rod, like any father would do. But my favor will not be taken from him as I took it from Saul, whom I removed from your sight. Your house and your kingdom will continue before me[b] for all time, and your throne will be secure forever."' 2 Sam. 7:11-16.

I have seen preemptive offering or giving also in the secular world. If you work in real estate or some other business transactions requiring buying and selling, there is a term called motivated seller. That means the seller is eager to close the transaction. However, in some cases, you would have to find out what would motivate the seller to close the transaction with you.

Some years ago at an advertising billboard camp that I attended, a land agent shared a story with us. His job was to secure land leases with landlords so that his company could build advertising billboards on the land. On one occasion, the landlord refused to deal. He would not allow billboards on his land. However, during their conversation, he discovered that the man needed a pickup truck for his son going to college and didn't have funds for it. The agent structured this into a deal. The company bought him the pickup truck, and they got a deal.

Personally, when it comes to giving to God and principles that I find in the Bible, I am very radical in implementing them as you can tell. Because I know Jesus is real, and He can never lie, I put Him on the spot. About two years ago, I implemented the law of preemptive giving. I sold all the stock investments that I had control over and gave them to God. One of the reasons why I did these things is to let God know that money has no hold on me. He owns me and my money. He could demand it whenever He wants.

The reward of that preemptive giving is still coming in. One of them was a major investment that I had never thought about. It's astronomically more than what I gave. He also blessed me with so many ideas for the next five to ten years. The return was not right away, though. It took a bit. Yours could be right away or not. Sometimes you may even second guess yourself if you took the right decision. One thing with God though is that He never forgets. He would not owe you.

Action Item.

1. Make a list of needs in my church or ministry that I could meet.

2. God wants souls to be saved. I can regularly contribute to missionary outreaches.

3. Are there other areas that touches God's heart that I could give towards?

Chapter 21

Law of Faithfulness Over Little

"...You have been faithful in handling this small amount, so now I will give you many more responsibilities. Let's celebrate together!"'Matt. 25:23.

There are many people today who hate their work. They hate going to work. The work frustrates them. Work hours, environment, colleagues, bosses, and of course, the pay are just some of the frustrations that some experience at their place of work. Many do not let this affect their service or work performance. But, for others, it reflects in the way they handle their work. Some while away time, falsify records, steal, and some even sabotage systems because of their frustration. What we fail to realize is that God allows us to be in situations that would shape and prepare us for our own. While the work you are currently in probably is not most use of your talent, the law of faithfulness over little requires that you treat it as your own.

There are some skills you would need when you run your own

outfit that you must learn where you are. Continuous and faithful repetition no matter how boring, would enable you to hone your skills in that area and make you ready when your time comes. In fact, Jesus states emphatically in Luke 16:12 that the first requirement to getting your own is being faithful in the little you currently do for another person. He said if you are not faithful over little things, you would not be faithful over big things.

Financial success is a habit. If you cannot form a good habit that would make you successful with little resources, that habit would not just manifest suddenly when you need it. You may say there is absolutely no benefit to being diligent with your work where you are. I disagree. One benefit you could gain from working for someone is accountability and structure. Working for someone else would demand that you become accountable and that you are structured. Both skills are needed when you are running your own organization with no one to tell you what to do.

In the bible, we were told of Joseph. He was to be a prime minister with rulership over all of Egypt. Still, prior to this, he managed the affairs of the house of Potiphar as a slave. Then when he had the opportunity to sleep with his boss's wife he turned it down remaining faithful. He was wrongly accused and thrown in prison for it. "No good deeds go unpunished."

Surprisingly, Joseph went on to become a successful administrator of the prison where he was. This is still not the big dream that God gave him about 13 years earlier. All the same, God thought the prison was the best way to prepare the future prime minister of the world's superpower. Imagine if the candidate for the President of the United States has these as their job experience? God was allowing him to be tested, pressured, and his emotions and temperament tried. Nonetheless, he stood his ground, and then God rewarded him with his lifelong dream. More untold riches than he could ever have.

Personally, I have been in several uncomfortable positions where God had allowed me to be in. There are some career positions that had underutilized my potentials and skills. Yet, I stuck with them and did my work with enthusiasm. I always look at the bigger picture of God's hand at work. I have learned several skills that have been invaluable for me in launching several ventures. I have also developed an original approach to solving problems because of these positions. Besides, I made friends along the way.

There are chances that your workplace was not as precarious as the palace of King Saul, where King David worked. Just in case you have forgotten, his boss tried to pin him to the wall twice with a spear. Yet, he learned palace protocols and administration from that position. Accordingly, after he was found faithful, God gave him that throne. Be faithful over little so God can give you your own.

Action Item.

1. What value can I bring to my current work environment?

2. What skills can I learn from my current work environment?

3. How can I be faithful over other things in my care?

PART IV:
BUSINESS LAWS

I discussed why building a business is the first cornerstone to becoming rich as the Bible reveals. I also enumerate laws that could allow you to be ahead of your competitors in your business.

CHAPTER 22

LAW OF BUILDING A BUSINESS FIRST

"Develop your business first before building your house."TLB Proverbs 24:27.

When the effect of the COVID-19 pandemic continued to destroy the economic wellbeing of many lives and businesses, many governments around the world began to take unprecedented actions. The European Union approved over $857 billion in stimulus package.[8] The U.S. also passed a $2 Trillion COVID-19 stimulus bill. The breakdown is below.

Category	Total Amount	Share of the Package
Individuals / Families	$603.7 billion	30%
Big Business	$500.0 billion	25%
Small Business	$377.0 billion	19%

Category	Total Amount	Share of the Package
State and Local Government	$340.0 billion	17%
Public Services	$179.5 billion	9%

Figure 4. Stimulus Package Breakdown.[9]

If you noticed in the table above, almost half (44%) of the package went to businesses. While qualifying individuals received a maximum of $1,200 per individual, companies under the small business category could receive up to $10 million in forgivable loans provided that some criteria were met. In fact, at least a company deemed critical to maintaining national security received $17 billion.[10]

Owning businesses is crucial to attaining financial independence especially during the pandemic and even beyond. This is one of the financial truths that Jesus taught me about getting rich. He told me to build my business first before the pleasure that I desire. This formed my financial decisions on many fronts.

In other to achieve this, I made some lifestyle changes. When I had opportunities to buy new cars, I stuck with one since I travel by train to and from work. I live in the city to keep the cost low. Though I love gadgets, I shunned opportunities to buy the latest phones. I used my phones until they drop dead. I took short road trips with the family instead of huge vacations. Majority of the income that I earned, I plowed back into my businesses. Though, I must say that it is not an easy proposition when you are married with kids. Sometimes I have to compromise a bit so we can still have fun on our journey to becoming rich.

Meanwhile, as you can see in the stimulus package example at the opening of this chapter, the United States of America and many societies around the world are built on and around businesses. In fact, in America, all sources of income are not equal. There are preferential treatments for income sources. There are several tax breaks for those who own businesses that employees would not receive. For example, if a single person built a business and earned $100,000 from that business, he would get to keep more money in his pocket than a doctor or other professional who earned this same amount. The business is able to deduct the cost of earning that $100,000 while the employee would not be able to deduct as much.

The wealthy are building businesses, creating enterprises where the poor go to shop. This returns the money from the poor back again into the coffers of the wealthy, making them richer and the poor poorer. You are making someone rich every day with the choices you make. Starbucks, Amazon, Facebook, Google, are getting rich off of you. Why not you? When would it be your turn to be paid?

Buying a house has always been the American dream. It is still being marketed as such. In fact, for years, a house has been called an asset. The saying is that it is the biggest investment you would ever make. We all found that not to be true. A house is not an investment or an asset. It is a liability. As Robert Kiyosaki would say, anything that takes money out of your pocket is not an asset. It is a liability. I agree. You pay mortgage on your house to the mortgage company. Your house is only an asset if it pays you money. Maybe if you use it for Airbnb.

If you are reading this and you already have a business, great. Can you afford to take a vacation from your business, and it would still continue to function? Does your business always require your presence? If you answered "No" to the first and "Yes" to the second, you don't yet have a business. You have a job. You are self-employed. Microsoft is a business. While the founder Bill Gates has retired, the business has only continued to grow in leaps and bounds. Starbucks is also a business. It does not require the founder Howard Schultz before it can function. However, you can also turn your self-employment job into a business. I will give you a little crash course on how.

Many small businesses start their life through an entrepreneur who acts as a technician because they do almost everything in the business. They are the embodiment of the business. It could even be their personality that sustains the business. Maybe that sounds like you? To turn your self-employment (business) into a business in the real sense, you need to introduce systems into your operations. You need to standardize every activity that you do. Develop standard operating procedures that could train even a high school dropout if needed to do what you do. Leave only the most crucial for your attention. Then slowly grow yourself out of this as well and delegate to someone else. If you have multiple locations, ensure the same top-notch customer service is standardized across your locations. You can get more specific information from

The E-Myth Revisited: Why Most Small Businesses Don't Work and What to Do About It by Michael E. Gerber.

Action Item.

1. I should consider building a business.

2. I need to invest in getting as much information as possible for the business.

3. I must turn my self-employment into a business.

4. I need to read *The E-Myth Revisited: Why Most Small Businesses Don't Work and What to Do About It by Michael E. Gerber,* for additional information.

CHAPTER 23

LAW OF PRIME MOVER

"When the Spirit of truth comes, he will guide you into all truth. He will not speak on his own but will tell you what he has heard. **He will tell you about the future***. John 16:13.*

As a Christian, one of the benefits you should have because of your affiliation with Jesus is being a prime mover or the first to bring an idea to fruition. The financial law of being a prime mover could quicken your journey to becoming financially independent. It would give you an advantage that makes you light years ahead of your competitor. You would be able to dominate your industry before anyone else.

How would your financial life have been impacted if you were the one that came up with the idea for Facebook, Amazon or Apple? They were primer movers. They were the first to bring to fruition ideas that have revolutionized our world. Consequentially, their owners are worth several billions of dollars.

How would you like to know the next trend in fashion, in

technology, entertainment, medical advancement, and launch ahead? Do you know God is able to do it? Do you know Jesus promised it and wants to do it for you?

Every human being only knows what they know. They have limited knowledge. They don't know what they don't know. That's a natural human being. You see, God who is Omniscient i.e. the person who knows all things, does share some of His omniscient abilities with His children. In Deuteronomy. 29:29, it says, *"The secret things belong to the LORD our God, but the things revealed belong to us and to our children forever..."*

Jesus told us that we have the ability to know what is to come by His Holy Spirit. *"When the Spirit of truth comes, he will guide you into all truth. He will not speak on his own but will tell you what he has heard. **He will tell you about the future**." John 16:13.* When you are able to introduce what no eye has ever seen, what no ear has ever heard, or what has never entered into the imagination of anyone, but revealed to you by Jesus as indicated in I Corinthians 2:9, you would be a prime mover. I took this Bible verse literally to heart and I pursued it.

About two years ago, as I laid down on my bed, the Lord Jesus whispered in my ears that old trends would be making a comeback. A month or two later, the fidget spinner toy made a comeback and hit the scene. It exploded, generating a lot of sales and making many rich. Everywhere you turned, people started making fidget spinners until it died out. Those who caught the trend late still have inventories unsold. A Christian who is a prime mover would have taken advantage of this.

Often times, I receive investment ideas in church. First, my church is saturated with the prophetic atmosphere, so anyone just starting out in the prophetic or desiring the prophetic could very easily pick up prophetic signals. I believe this is largely due to the fact that one of the dominant grace of my Resident Pastor is the prophetic.

This prophetic grace manifests in several dimensions and forms. It could come via words of knowledge, words of wisdom, visions and then prophetic utterances.

In one instance, I remembered that I was in church for one of our mid-week meetings. In fact, it was a prayer meeting. In one of the prayer sessions, as I closed my eyes, immediately the Lord flashed a vision before me a vision of a young black painter leaning against the wall. I recognized the person because I had recently invested in one of his paintings a few weeks earlier. Seeing it again, I know there is something the Lord is telling me in that direction.

Because this book is about what Jesus taught me about financial independence, sometimes in visions flashed before me such as the one above, the Lord would tell me right away what it meant by allowing my mind to connect the dots to understand it. Other times I would have to manually investigate. That was what I did with regards to this vision. As I scour through my emails for information from the company that I had invested through earlier I found out a pleasant surprise. The company had sent me an invitation to RSVP for another offering of a black painter. He was leaning against the wall. He was once overlooked, but now his works are taking off and appreciating at a phenomenal rate compared to others. That vision was the Lord was giving me an advance notice to get in ahead of others.

Again, few weeks to the time of writing this section, the Lord Jesus showed me an invention He wants me to make. He showed me the parts, how it works, and the sales it would generate. I have searched everywhere online to see whether such a thing exists and I have not found any. The idea is so simple that I wondered why anyone has never thought of it. I intend to pursue it fully by the grace of God and perhaps write about it in subsequent books. I intend to be a prime mover in that direction.

Nevertheless, it is possible that the idea that the Lord dropped in your spirit is not profitable right away. Do not worry. If it is the Lord who gave you the idea, it would eventually be profitable. Stay there. Remember the story of Isaac. God told him to remain in the land where there was famine. Everything was dead. It did not look promising, but God told him to invest. However, by the end of the year, he was insanely wealthy, so much that he was richer than the entire nation. Also, it is possible that what God told you to do is in variance with what others are doing. Ignore them and stay with yours. Recall that you have God's backing, and anything He backs succeeds.

Action Item

1. I must be conscious that I have an advantage over everyone who does not know Jesus because of His Holy Spirit.

2. I must take time to pray to God to give me prime mover ideas.

3. I must have my phone or paper and pen ready record whenever God drop the ideas.

4. I must observe my dreams for clues on what the Lord wants me to do.

5. I must practice the financial law of meditation.

Chapter 24

Law of Excellence

"Then this Daniel distinguished himself above the governors and satraps, because an excellent spirit was in him; and the king gave thought to setting him over the whole realm." Daniel 6:3. KJV.

When I originally started writing this portion, an alert came on my phone from the New York Times. It says, "Basquiat Painting Is Sold for $110.5 Million at Auction." It was a 1982 painting of a skull. It goes further to say that it is the most paid at an auction for any American Artist. "He is now in the league of Francis Bacon and Pablo Picasso.[11] A little bit over two years later, when I would revisit this portion to finish it off, the Lord told me specifically that one of the problems preventing many Christians from becoming rich was lack of excellence. He began to bring to remembrance sectors of the economy and comparing the output of what Christian companies produced compared to secular companies. It is a night and day difference regarding touch of excellence. Secular companies were light years ahead. Ask yourself this question. Were there other artists that painted in 1982? Yes.

Were there Christians among them? You bet. But only Jean-Michel Basquiat's skull painting, called *Untitled*, was regarded as the most excellent with a very rich reward.

In several sectors, many Christians' actions demonstrates that they expect as soon as they invoke the name of the Lord to be a part of their business, He would take care of the rest. This cannot be further from the truth. The world goes for excellence and would pay top dollar for excellence. Why do Apple products have a large following around the world despite their prices? Their customers believe their products are made with excellence.

You see, for the most part, people buy with emotions. We purchase many things, especially gadgets, because of perception and the way they make us feel. You probably would not hear from an Apple customer that they bought an Apple product because it was cheaper. There are far cheaper cellular phones in the market than the iPhone. However, the original visionary leader of the Apple company, the late Steve Jobs, was obsessed with excellence. He was particular about every detail of the product his company produces and has passed this on to his successors.

I mentioned that we usually buy things based on emotion, especially if they are not necessities. Here is what the Japanese billionaire who paid $110.5 million for Basquiat's *Untitled* painting had to say. *"I am happy to announce that I just won this masterpiece,"* he said in the post. *"When I first encountered this painting, I was struck with so much excitement and gratitude for my love of art. I want to share that experience with as many people as possible."*[12]

One person who modeled excellence in the bible and was richly rewarded was Daniel. The bible tells us that he had an excellent spirit. This meant that excellence was not just an act for him. It had become a part of who he was. Because of this excellent spirit, which was reflected in the way he handled his affairs, he became wealthy in Babylon, not minding that he got there as a slave. Excellence has nothing to do with your color, race or gender. He was regularly called upon as an expert on complex matters. For us to know that it was not a fluke, he served four kings in Babylon and was richer with each one:

Nebuchadnezzar - *Daniel 2:48. Then the king appointed Daniel to a high position and gave him many valuable gifts. He made Daniel ruler over the whole province of Babylon, as well as chief over all his wise men.*

Belshazzar - *Daniel 5:29. Then at Belshazzar's command, Daniel was dressed in purple robes, a gold chain was hung around his neck, and he was proclaimed the third highest ruler in the kingdom.*

Darius - *Daniel 6:3. Daniel soon proved himself more capable than all the other administrators and high officers. Because of Daniel's great ability, the king made plans to place him over the entire empire),*

Cyrus - *Daniel 6:28. So Daniel prospered during the reign of Darius and the reign of Cyrus the Persian.*

In each administration, Daniel rose higher and higher. It got to the point that the king wanted to appoint him as the overall prime minister of the entire realm.

Look around you. How many Christian businesses are operated with excellence when compared to secular businesses or companies in the same sector? Consequently, lots of money that should find its way into kingdom coffers is funding ungodly values. Would you dare to change this by modeling excellence? A customer may mistakenly visit a business once but may likely not return if they found excellence elsewhere.

I read many stories of the late Michael Jackson especially about how he would go over songs and certain dance steps hundreds of hours until he nailed them to perfection. No wonder his album is still bestselling years after his death. He's still being financially rewarded for it.

The same could be said of Michael Jordan when he was active as a basketball player. He was in the gym before everyone and left late. Despite that he was gifted, he would spend thousands of hours practicing. It paid off on many occasions, especially when he nails game-winning shots. He also became a billionaire.

The financial law of excellence is inevitable in our world. That is what the world craves. Even a mediocre wants an exceptional product and service.

Action Item.

1. I need to ask God for the spirit of excellence.

2. I need to exemplify excellence in all that I do.

3. I need to identify and find out what other secular competitors are doing excellently well that I could emulate.

CHAPTER 25

LAW OF SERVICE

---

*But don't act like them. If you want to be great, you must
be the servant of all the others. Matthew 20:26.*

What is one thing that J.K. Rowling and Jeff Bezos have in common? They became billionaires by serving lots of people with their ideas. J.K. Rowling became a billionaire with the Harry Potter series though she had given much away since then. Jeff Bezos also serves more people with Amazon.

According to Rabbi Daniel Lapin in his book *Business Secrets From The Bible, Spiritual Success Strategies for Financial Abundance,* we must understand that money or financial reward is one of God's way of compensating those who serve humanity with their ideas. The more people you serve or bring value to their lives, the greater your financial reward. We see this with Jeff Bezos (Amazon), Bill Gates (Microsoft), founder of Chick-Fil-A, etc.

Service in the context of financial laws is simply solving people's problems with your solution. Millions of people needed fast shipping, excellent customer service, and a centralized and safe place to do their shopping. Amazon provided that for them. So they continued to reward the company with their wallets.

Another case in point, in 2019, it was noted that Chick-Fil-A went from being the seventh-largest restaurant chain in the United States to becoming the third.[13] Chick-Fil-A was founded by Samuel Truett Cathy, a Christian, who believes in not opening on Sunday so that his employees could go to church. The majority of other restaurant chains like KFC its chicken competitor, opened on Sundays. Yet, in the same year, according to the Washington Post, average sales per Chick-fil-A location was more than three times that of KFC.[14]

So, considering that Chick-Fil-A is usually picketed against because of their conservative values, why did customers reward Chick-Fil-A with their hard-earned cash with sales up 17% in 2019? According to David Portalatin, a food industry expert cited by Laura Reiley, who wrote the report, "the principal reason for Chick-fil-A is the customer experience." In his own words, *"The level of customer satisfaction is highly differentiated from many of their fast-food peers." Chick-fil-A's customer service is legendary, prompting rafts of memes enumerating real and imagined over-the-top polite employee interactions."*

Did you see what was used to describe the customer service experience? Legendary! Imagine if your customers describe their experience in your business to others with such words? You would certainly have more than your hands full every day. No wonder our Lord Jesus said the way to the top is through service.

Again, when you use your creativity to help others, they benefit. God has made it in such a way that the more people you serve in your business, the wealthier you become. It also means that if you don't serve anyone, you remain poor.

Does this also apply to a preacher? Yes. If what you believe is the concept of where "two or three are gathered," then expect to receive only the financial blessings that come from serving only a handful. However, if you believe in serving more people even beyond your primary congregation, with what they need, then expect big financial blessings. It's a financial law that continues to prove true.

Chances are you've read the book *The Purpose Driven Life* by Rick Warren. Rick Warren, as you may know, is the Pastor of Saddleback Church in Saddleback, California. A large congregation by any measure. However, the success of his book *The Purpose Driven Life*, which has sold 50 million copies in more than 85 languages,[15] is even mind-boggling. The success of the book, according to him, allowed him to pay back 25 years of salaries to his church. He also tithes over 90% of his income.[16] What does this mean? He served more people more than his primary constituency with a solution that they needed. It resonated with at least about 50 million people of which I am one. He also got wealthier in the process.

The mammoth success of Warren's book, while uncommon, proves that the law of service in becoming rich works. So, I ask you? Who are you going to serve with your gift? Remember that the way out of financial lack is through service.

Action Item.

1. I need to take an inventory of what gift I can use to serve others.

2. I need to make exceptional, legendary customer satisfaction a normal in my business.

3. The more people whose needs I can meet through service, the more rewarding it would be.

CHAPTER 26

LAW OF SELLING

"Jesus replied, "Anyone who drinks this water will soon become thirsty again. But those who drink the water I give will never be thirsty again. It becomes a fresh, bubbling spring within them, giving them eternal life." "Please, sir," the woman said, "give me this water! Then I'll never be thirsty again, and I won't have to come here to get water."
John 4:13-15.

I almost forgot a very important law that Jesus taught me, the law of selling. I know you may say, but I don't sell anything, and I don't want to get involved in any buying and selling but hear me out. We are all sellers. It may not be in the way you have thought, but you have sold and would continue to sell.

Let me break it down for you. Selling is basically trying to win someone over to your side to accept your offer with some persuasion. The ideal situation is for both parties to win. What our Lord Jesus Christ came to do when He came to the world was to basically sell us the benefits of accepting Him. Some of the benefits of accepting Him include going to heaven, having our names in the book of life, being connected to the Father, living an abundant life, being rich, putting

Satan under our feet, etc. What do we give in exchange for this? Our soul. It is the only currency acceptable. The brutal alternative, according to Jesus, if anyone refuses to accept Him, is condemnation and God's fierce judgment. *"And anyone who believes in God's Son has eternal life. Anyone who doesn't obey the Son will never experience eternal life but remains under God's angry judgment" (John 3:36).*

Thus, all through His entire short life on earth, everywhere Jesus went, He was busy selling this idea. Depending on who He was meeting, He presented His messages customized for that audience. For example, when He met the Samaritan woman at the well, who had a problem keeping a husband, He presented the message as someone who needed a drink of water from the well. That way, He began to reel her into His real message. By the time He introduced Himself as the Messiah, she didn't know what hit her. She accepted Him and told everyone about Him (John 4:1-42).

Jesus also used the selling method to get Peter's attention. He borrowed His boat to preach, and after He was done, He identified what Peter needed. Peter had fished all night but caught nothing. So, Jesus gave Him an offer He couldn't refuse. He helped him (Peter) to get what he needed. Peter caught so much fish that his net began to break. He called his partners from other boats to join in to haul the great catch. They did, but their boats also started sinking because of the great catch. The deal was sealed. In fact, the bible said the fishermen left everything and followed Jesus (Luke 5:1-11). What a Salesman whose stuff works!

How does that apply to you? As I mentioned earlier, you are already selling. If you are a married man, chances are you sold your wife on who you are and who she is before she became your spouse? If you have ever been interviewed, you sold the interviewers on what you bring to their organization. They were convinced of the benefits you enumerated, that was why you were hired. Now, what you need to master is transferring this skill to becoming rich. You would need to sell investors your ideas if you need to bring them into your business. If you are selling physical products in a brick and mortar store, you would need to learn how to do that. If you would be selling online, the skill you'd need to master or perhaps outsource is copywriting. You must be able to convince customers who don't see you about the benefits of paying for your service or products through written words.

If there was something that I detested before, it was selling. I guess I have seen some professions that take advantage of their customers and clients too many times. It was a one-sided win. All that mattered to them was winning at all costs. They do not care about their clients.

However, Jesus taught me that it was inevitable if I want to become rich. I need to learn how to sell in a win-win situation. I then began to master this art. I have raised a considerable amount of funds for projects because of my ability to sell. When I communicate the gospel, I am selling.

The basic tenets of selling are the same. You must find out what your clients or customers need. They may know it at the time or not. Then present it to the buyer in a way that it satisfies what's in it for me. For example, we never knew we needed an iPad until Steve Jobs presented it to us. Take a look again at the story of Jesus and the woman at the well. She didn't know she needed a savior until Jesus presented it to her. First, Jesus said, I will give you water that when you drink it, you will never thirst anymore. That's what's in it for her. *Jesus replied, "Anyone who drinks this water will soon become thirsty again. But those who drink the water I give will never be thirsty again. It becomes a fresh, bubbling spring within them, giving them eternal life." "Please, sir," the woman said, "give me this water! Then I'll never be thirsty again, and I won't have to come here to get water"* (John 4:13-15).

Now, the woman was more interested. Jesus then went further to tell her He was the messiah and proved it by telling her, her past and present. That was the unique selling point. The deal was sealed. The woman went on to become an evangelist for Jesus and got the entire town to come out and listen to Him. The product Jesus was presenting was proof positive. *28 The woman left her water jar beside the well and ran back to the village, telling everyone, 29 "Come and see a man who told me everything I ever did! Could he possibly be the Messiah?"*The customer review from a satisfied customer, the Samaritan woman, was what was needed to win the entire village for Jesus. They even persuaded Him to stay for two days. *39 Many Samaritans from the village believed in Jesus because the woman had said, "He told me everything I ever did!" 40 When they came out to see him, they begged him to stay in their village. So he stayed for two days, 41 long enough for many more to hear his message and believe. 42 Then they said to the woman, "Now we believe, not just because of what you told us, but because we have heard him ourselves. Now we know that he is indeed the Savior of the world."*You also need a unique selling point when you want to sell. What makes you better than others? In addition, you also need satisfied customers to spread the word of how good your product or service is.

There are lots of good books on selling that could really help you in doing this regardless of your aversion for selling. A great book that I have read is *Sell Or Be Sold* by Grant Cardone.

Action Item.

1. I need to master the art of selling.

2. I need to read books that teach about selling such as Sell Or Be Sold by Grant Cardone, Sales Dogs by Blair Singer, or other books on sales.

PART V:
PARTNERSHIP LAWS

I f you would succeed in any business or venture, you need the right team, partners, and associations. In this part, I discuss the financial laws that could give you success when building a team and show you how to speed up your journey to riches with a team, etc.

CHAPTER 27

LAW OF BETTING ON YOURSELF

> *"...is like a treasure that a man discovered hidden in a field. In his excitement, he hid it again and sold everything he owned to get enough money to buy the field...is like a merchant on the lookout for choice pearls. When he discovered a pearl of great value, he sold everything he owned and bought it!" Matthew 13:44-46.*

Some years ago, a brother who was a member of my church at the time approached me for financial assistance. It was for thousands of dollars. We had some discussions back and forth regarding what he wanted to do. He had an idea for a particular toy that would aid toddlers in walking. It sounded like a brilliant idea. What he needed were the funds to take the idea through patent, produce a prototype and hopefully market it to companies who could sell it to the public on a large scale. I studied the proposal, and I then asked him what his contribution to the venture was? He said he did not have enough money. The little check he receives from the government monthly wasn't enough. So he could not afford to contribute anything financially aside from the idea he was bringing to the table. Though he touted with enthusiasm how brilliant the idea was, and how excellent his invention was when compared to what was already in the market, I had no option but to turn him down.

Here is why, which is why the law is important. There are so many things wrong with this picture. The brother did not have anything at risk. Anyone could have an idea. In fact, everyone has an idea. Ideas are a dime and a dozen. However, the majority of ideas would not work in real life because of various reasons such as timing, regulations, resources, location, etc.

To convince an investor to invest in your idea, the law of financial independence demands that you put your skin in the game. For the brother persuading me to invest in his venture, without his money at stake, which could elicit pain from him, it would be easy for him to work away at any time he wants. Also, if he was convinced that this was a gold mine, he should be able to bet on himself.

Successful inventors and business owners who attain financial independence do not only bring ideas, but they are willing to bet on themselves, put their meager fortune at risk because they believe in the vision of the idea. Many have slept in cars to accomplish their ideas. The great filmmaker, studio owner, actor and producer Tyler took his entire life savings of $12,000 to pay for a theater for his play. That endeavor still bombed. Only about thirty people showed up, which were just people he knew. Today the rest is history as he built on successes upon successes.

If the path of your financial independence involves great ideas, and you require investors or partners, make sure that you also have skin in the game beyond just your ideas. Taking an equal or significant risk in proportion to your net worth is one of the signs that convinces investors that you are serious about your idea, and you believe in it.

I have raised some significant funds requiring partners and

investors. Aside from bringing ideas to the table, I also bring funds to the table. Investors are not actually investing in the project. They are investing in me. They are betting on me. If the deal is good enough, the law of financial independence requires that you bet on yourself.

Our Lord told a parable regarding this in the book of Matthew 13:44-46. I will rephrase it this way. *.is like an idea that a man discovered. In his excitement, he hid it again and sold everything he owned to get enough money to invest in the idea. "...is like a merchant on the lookout for choice investments. When he discovered an investment of great value, he sold everything he owned and bought it!*

Action Item.

1. Revisit my ideas that had failed because I didn't bet on myself.

2. Outline plan to do things differently.

CHAPTER 28

LAW OF DIVINE HELPERS

"The following day John was again standing with two of his disciples. As Jesus walked by, John looked at him and declared, "Look! There is the Lamb of God!" When John's two disciples heard this, they followed Jesus." John 1:35-37.

*There was a young Hebrew man with us in the prison...
And everything happened just as he had predicted...
Then Pharaoh said to Joseph, "Since God has revealed the meaning of the dreams to you, clearly no one else is as intelligent or wise as you are. You will be in charge of my court, and all my people will take orders from you. Only I, sitting on my throne, will have a rank higher than yours."
Genesis 41:12-13,39-40.*

One of the financial laws Jesus taught me for becoming rich is the law of divine helpers. He taught me that to become rich or financially independent, I must be helped by someone.

There is a false narrative or description out there when you read the biography of several wealthy individuals. Sometimes the reporters write that their source of wealth as self-made when differentiating from those who inherited their wealth. The reality in life is this. No one is self-made. Everyone who became rich or financially independent was helped by someone. Someone gave them an opportunity. Someone gave them a leg up. Someone along the line might have introduced them to another person who enables their dream to be possible. For some folks, it is those who worked for and with them. For others, it is their spouse. Still, others could be a government grant or even a loan from the bank. There is absolutely nobody who became wealthy who wasn't helped.

I like using the word divine helpers. This is when God positions some people along your path to enable you to accomplish your goals. There are references whose role is to recommend you. Such was the Chief Butler, who recommended Joseph to King Pharaoh. John the Baptist also did this for our Lord Jesus Christ when he told everyone. In fact, Andrew and John (the closest disciple to Jesus) were disciples of John the Baptist. They left and followed Jesus based on John's recommendation.

Some notable stories I remember of a divine helper was that of President Barack Obama. He was largely unknown nationally until July 27, 2004. He was just a state senator. However, the Democratic presidential candidate John Kerry selected him to deliver the keynote address at the democratic convention. That night changed his political fortunes forever. Four years later, he became the President of the United States of America. John Kerry was his divine helper.

In addition to references who recommend you being divine helpers, investors who invest in you and your vision are also divine helpers. Many women who were disciples of Jesus fulfilled this role. Notable among them were two sisters named Mary and Martha, and Salome.

Some other divine helpers that you may need could be warriors who go to fight for your interests, whether at the city hall or in court. Jonathan did this for King David. There are also spiritual guides who pray for you and encourage you. Prophet Samuel did this for King Saul. Divine helpers come in various ways fulfilling differing roles. Identify yours. This is a requirement for financial independence.

Action Item.

1. I need to look within my circle and identify those sent to help me.

2. I need to know that help could come from anyone.

CHAPTER 29

LAW OF RIGHT ASSOCIATION

"Walk with the wise and become wise; associate with fools and get in trouble." Proverbs 13:20.

In the bible verse above, the Bible tells us that the companion of the wise would be wise, but that of fools would be destroyed. We can also apply the same that the companion of the rich would be rich. What happens to the companion of the poor?

Have you noticed that when taking a walk with a friend, spouse or colleague, automatically the pace levels off whereby both of you would adjust to the same pace? That is also the case for the financial laws of right association. Your bosom friends cannot be those without a wealthy mindset if you want to be financially independent or wealthy. They cannot be those who do not have a positive attitude towards money. They can't be those who believe in taking from the rich and redistributing to the poor as a wealth strategy.

When it comes to the foremost tech companies in the U.S., you will find at least one thing in common. Many of the CEOs or board members have either worked together or have some things that bring them together. They usually love to hang out only within their company or circle and even rotate the association and work circle. For example, Elon Musk, who is the current CEO of Tesla, the Motor Company, and Space X, founded Paypal along with Peter Thiel (Palantir Technologies), Yu Pan (Kiwi Crate), and others. On a larger scale, the leading hub of technology innovation is Silicon Valley in California. Almost everyone in the technology industry has a connection to Silicon Valley. The same goes for Hollywood, where like-minded people who are interested in movie and television associate. Boston, Massachusetts, is also the hub of mutual funds. Anyone serious about a career in the stock market would have an association with Wall Street in New York. I could go on and on, but you get the picture.

The right association matters regarding becoming rich. You don't have to dismiss everyone. You can implement the model Jesus used in qualifying people for access to Him and sensitive information. First, Jesus had the crowd, which are tens of thousands that followed Him. Out of that crowd, He selected seventy that He trusted with special tasks. They go to villages He couldn't go and preach for Him. Out of this seventy, He has the twelve disciples that He keeps closer. These are the folks that He explains his teaching to in details. Often He would tell them things and warn them not to share the information with others. Further, He had a special trio of Peter, James and John. From His twelve disciples, these are the most trusted confidants that He takes on the most sensitive meetings, such as on the Mount of Transfiguration. You would think that is all? No. He has that special person that is the most trusted of all out of the trio. It is John. He is the one He told about Judas Iscariot's betrayal. He is also the one He handed over His mother to for care when He was on the cross.

I went through the above filter to give you a model for classifying your association. Because someone is a Christian doesn't mean they should have an equal level of access to you as others. It has to be the right association. We are heavily influenced by the people we spend the most time with. We are easily swayed by people whose opinions we value even when they are flat out wrong.

Action Item.

1. Evaluate those I associate with and found out their views on becoming rich.

2. Identify the covenant association that I need to invest in.

3. Think about the last good investment opportunity that I missed. Who influenced me wrongly?

4. I need to visit www.betterinvesting.org to find out local stock investment clubs near me.

5. For real estate investment, I need to visit https://www.biggerpockets.com/ or www.reiclub.com for like-minded individuals.

CHAPTER 30

LAW OF IDENTIFYING THE COVENANT PERSON

L et me discuss a concept that would really impact your life regarding the right person or right association. I had originally included it in the law of right association, but I believe it should be given more in-depth publicity. The law of identifying the covenant person in your life is very critical for your financial success, as you would soon see.

We are equal in the sight of the Lord, but we operate in different graces. We have been sent to do different tasks to impact our world for the Lord. However, you would soon discover that in God's infinite wisdom, He has designated some people to have a covenant with. Those are the people through whom He carries out major activities on earth. For example, out of the entire world, when God was about to destroy the world with a flood, He chose Noah and established a covenant with him. Everyone who associated with him was saved from the flood. God also chose Abraham and established a covenant with him. One of the promises He gave him was that He would bless everyone who blesses him and curse everyone who does. Lot, who was his nephew, associated with him and became rich because of this. Consequently,when Lot left Abraham, he lost everything.

God also chose Jacob. Laban, Jacob's uncle, confessed that it was because of Jacob that he became rich.

Soon after Rachel had given birth to Joseph, Jacob said to Laban, "Please release me so I can go home to my own country. Let me take my wives and children, for I have earned them by serving you, and let me be on my way. " "Please listen to me," Laban replied. "I have become wealthy, for the LORD has blessed me because of you. Tell me how much I owe you. Whatever it is, I'll pay it." Jacob replied, "You know how hard I've worked for you, and how your flocks and herds have grown under my care. You had little indeed before I came, but your wealth has increased enormously. The LORD has blessed you through everything I've done. But now, what about me? When can I start providing for my own family? Genesis 30:25-30.

Then He chose Joseph. The bible says that God was blessing Potiphar's house because of Joseph. *"From the day Joseph was put in charge of his master's household and property, the LORD began to bless Potiphar's household for Joseph's sake. All his household affairs ran smoothly, and his crops and livestock flourished. Gen 39:5."*

Why did I go this length to explain? You must identify your covenant person. You need to recognize the covenant person in your circle. Whenever you want to engage in an association or partnership, your first order of choice should be the covenant person. They may not have money, ideas or appear as smart as others. However, the grace of God on them would give you speed and guarantee the success you need. Without a covenant person, it might be an uphill battle. The covenant person is what the world calls a lucky person.

I did a financial management teaching sometime in my church when Jesus taught me how the concept of the covenant person works. The shortest route for a family to become rich is to identify the Joseph, David or Abraham in the family and support the person wholeheartedly. Identify the covenant person and let the family rally round that person to give them a leg up. You must understand that you are all on the same team and, with humility, raise up the hands of the covenant person. The covenant person could be the wife, husband, children, uncle, cousin, etc. Unfortunately, many families usually give their covenant person the left foot of fellowship. The covenant persons are usually often misunderstood because of their personality, approach and other qualities. This was the case with King David when he was young. The family never realized he was the savior of Israel. The king that God wants.

Let me emphasize again, whereas God loves everyone equally and has assigned each of us to a different purpose in the family or in life, there is usually a Joseph that God has inserted into each family or group. They are assigned the purpose of being the financial savior or the star of that family. God has no regard of persons as regards this. There could be other stars that would come after them in the family, but the Joseph must rise to the top first. *"God has sent me ahead of you to keep you and your families alive and to preserve many survivors." Gen 45:7.* A wise family should totally support this person as the family rises or falls on whether the person succeeds or not. This person should receive the maximum support so they could focus on what the Lord has sent them to do. If they are hated, chased away, rejected, you can be sure that family will not be financially successful until the Joseph is restored. There are scriptural and practical examples. The Josephs also know that without the support they can never succeed. It is both ways. No matter how gifted a person is, without the right support and environment, it is as if they are not gifted. Again, if you are a covenant person, you need to make sure that you treat the people the Lord has sent to help you well. You need them as much as they need you. Without the Chief Butler, Joseph would have rotted in an Egyptian prison.

Action Item.

1. I need to identify the covenant person in my circle.

2. I need to support the covenant person in my circle.

3. If I am the covenant person, I need to be humble in treating my enablers, supporters well.

PART VI:
INVESTMENT LAWS

You will make some investment decisions in your life in various attempts to build riches. In this section, I show you how to use biblical investment laws to your advantage. I also demonstrate practically how to use the little you have to build riches.

CHAPTER 31

LAW OF SEED TO THE SOWER & BREAD TO THE EATER

> *"Now he who supplies seed to the sower and bread for food will also supply and increase your store of seed and will enlarge the harvest of your righteousness." 2 Corinthians 9:10. NIV.*

> *"This most generous God who gives seed to the farmer that becomes bread for your meals is more than extravagant with you. He gives you something you can then give away, which grows into full-formed lives, robust in God, wealthy in every way, so that you can be generous in every way, producing with us great praise to God." 2 Corinthians. 9:10-11. MSG.*

Regarding finances, I believe there are two classes of people. It is not the rich and the poor. The two classes of people are the sower and the eater. Those who set aside to plant and those who eat everything. The folks who have an investment mentality and those with a consumer mentality. Your behavior determines which side you belong to.

If you noticed, nothing in these descriptions mentioned the rich and the poor. A poor person who sets aside something to invest is only poor temporarily. Eventually, he would leave that state and become rich. The same goes for the person who finds themselves in sudden riches but spends as if it's going out of style. They would eventually be poor. Have you observed that most lottery winners eventually end up becoming broke again and sometimes worse off? It is because they were not sowers. Money was not the cure. Ironically, money cannot invalidate financial laws.

If you are always sowing, which is investing what you earn, you would always have more. On the other hand, if you are always eating everything without setting anything aside to invest, you would only always have enough to eat or consume but not enough to grow into wealth.

Know this, your successful financial future would be dependent on setting aside something today. If you don't set something aside today, you have nothing waiting in the future. If you're not setting something aside today, you will likely work till you die. On the other hand, if you are setting aside to invest, no matter how little you earn, as a Christian, God would always ensure that you have enough to invest. Not only that, but He would also multiply what you have sown. Just as a grain of corn doesn't just produce a grain of corn at harvest, so also would be the seed of money that you set aside.

You can set aside between 2% -10% of your paycheck or whatever you are comfortable with initially for sowing. If you have your paycheck directly deposited into your account, you can set up an allotment for this amount to go to where you want it invested. If you receive physical cash or check, you can put the cash money in an envelope labeled **SEED** or **INVESTMENT.** This could then be directed to your investment of choice.

Some of the ways to invest it could be buying shares of stocks of any company you want. If the share price (not the value) is too high for you, you can sign up with companies that allow you to buy fractional shares for as little as one dollar. There are several companies that offer this. Some of them are M1 Finance, Stash, Robinhood, Stockpile, Fidelity, Public, etc. They have apps that can be downloaded.

Action Item.

1. Set aside between 2% -10% of my paycheck.

2. Invest my Seed. It could be in stocks, real estate, a business or whatsoever I choose.

3. Resist the urge to sell my assets to meet my immediate needs.

CHAPTER 32

LAW OF INVESTING IN YOURSELF

"Even though Jesus was God's Son, he learned obedience..." Hebrews 5:8." Study and be eager and do your utmost to present yourself to God... approved... correctly analyzing and accurately dividing..." 2 Timothy 2:15. AMPC.

In the law of creating value in chapter 40, I mentioned how I was able to create money by creating value. I tested this law with the T-shirt example that I gave. I also mentioned that you can't create value until you have invested in yourself. It is what you have invested in yourself that you could use to create value. Before I was able to create the T-shirt example that I mentioned, I had already invested in learning about it. I learned about designs, advertising, and all other information that goes along with it.

Unfortunately, in society today, so many people want to show up or show off without having paid the price. They are in a hurry for affluence. Since they are not rich, what they do is live a life that is not genuine. Sadly, Christians are also caught up in this web of faux lifestyle. They try to show the perception of wealth in various ways. Even so, with the advent of social media, there are so many with good photoshopping and video skills uploading video and pictures of a fake lifestyle of opulence. You can't blame social media. Before social media, many people have done this on a different scale. They go into debt to purchase luxury cars, houses, expensive bags, and watches to give the impression that they are rich. They are then stuck in a constant rat race to foot the bills. It is because they have failed to obey one of the fundamentals laws of becoming rich which is investing in themselves. If you were caught in that web before, I have a solution here for you.

To be successful in any discipline, Jesus taught us through the Bible that the individual must first invest a great deal in themselves. Have you ever wondered why you didn't read about Jesus from the age of twelve until thirty years when He began His ministry? It was on purpose. He was investing in Himself. He was studying. The bible tells us that He would be in the temple even at a young age asking questions with religious leaders. He did not bypass the process. God always allows people to go through the process. He is a structured person. Part of what Jesus learned, as the bible tells us in the book of Hebrews 5:8, was how to be obedient to the Father as a human being though He has the power to be independent of the Father. Isn't that what we also face as Christians? Though we will have always have options, we choose to submit to God.

Personally, I have spent over 10,000 hours, tens of thousands of dollars on courses, workshops, conferences, videos, books, group and so forth to learn financial education and the various disciplines that have a foothold in. They vary from oil and gas to billboard advertising, real estate, fine art, e-commerce, IPO, stocks, publishing, just to mention a few. These have helped me on how to analyze investment opportunities that come my way and in asset allocation. "*Study and* be eager *and* do your utmost to present yourself to God... approved...correctly analyzing *and* accurately dividing..." 2 Timothy 2:15. AMPC

I have equally invested uncountable hours in prayers, studying of the word, fasting, listening to messages and all other consecration that I mentioned so that I could have a deeper walk with Jesus and learn His ways. As you continue to invest in yourself both in the secular and the sacred, you would notice at least one benefit. You would be able to create value. Value is what brings money.

If you are a preacher, you may say that creating value to create money doesn't apply to you. It does. I have observed that preachers or servants of God who create value are the ones who are sought after and have schedules booked solid full of speaking engagements. These engagements, of course, translate to more income for them. Even if it doesn't translate to speaking engagements or book deals, when your congregation perceives you as someone who brings value to their lives, your perceived value in their eyes rises. This usually translates to the congregants extending more financial gifts to their leaders. However, this would not happen if you have not invested in yourself.

The bible tells us of John the Baptist, the forerunner of our Lord Jesus Christ. If you noticed, John stayed away hidden, investing in himself with prayers and fasting, secluded in the wilderness until the appropriate time. *"John grew up and became strong in spirit. And he lived in the wilderness until he began his public ministry to Israel"* *(Luke 1:80).*

Many Christians do not wait for their day of showing. They want to display publicly what they have not invested in privately. They want to jump the process. The process of self-investment could be painful at times. Think of self-investment as the tuition you are paying for your financial future. For example, the bible says after John was done, people came out from cities to listen to what he has to say in the desert. *"In those days John the Baptist came to the Judean wilderness and began preaching... People from Jerusalem and from all of Judea and all over the Jordan Valley went out to see and hear John"* *(Matthew 3:1,5).* He had value.

Let me encourage you to shut away from the noise of get rich quick schemes and invest in yourself. Investing in oneself is a requirement for Christians who are serious about becoming rich.

What steps should you take to discover how to invest in yourself? It's simple. First, you need to determine your goal, where you want to get to. For example, if you are trying to set up a T-shirt business, that would be the goal.

Second, determine how to get there. For my T-shirt business, I went on YouTube and listened to many successful T-shirt company owners for an overview and researched what is needed. I discovered that I would need a T-shirt printing company, know what niche I want to target, and know how to advertise on Facebook or other social media platform.

Next, you need to identify the strengths or skills that are needed for the business. Out of those skills, identify what you currently have. In my case, I already knew the likely audience that would be interested in those specific kinds of T-shirts. I also have a platform to notify them. However, I don't know how to market, especially to a broader audience.

So, that brings us to the next step—your weakness. My weakness was online marketing. Thus, I invested in both free and paid courses to learn online marketing portion.

Summarily, if you don't know how to invest in yourself, first determine your goal. Where do you want to go financially? Then, what business or venture do you want to get you there? Next, get an overview of the business. Then do a deep dive to identify the skills that are required. Finally, invest in those skills that are needed that you don't have.

Action Item.

1. I need to determine where I want to go financially.

2. I need to determine how to get there.

3. I need to get an overview of the business of venture

4. I need to do a deep dive to identify the skills that are required.

5. I need to invest in acquiring the required skills that are needed that I don't have.

CHAPTER 33

LAW OF LEVERAGING THE POWER OF LITTLE

"...Jesus took the five loaves and two fish, looked up toward heaven, and blessed them. Then, breaking the loaves into pieces, he gave the bread to the disciples, who distributed it to the people. They all ate as much as they wanted, and afterward, the disciples picked up twelve baskets of leftovers. About 5,000 men were fed that day, in addition to all the women and children!" Matthew 14:18-21.

D o you know how much you would have if you had invested $100 in Uber in 2009 and waited till 2020? Guess? By my calculation, it would have been $2 million. If you also had access to Facebook when it was starting out in 2004 and invested just $100, it would be worth between $1.8 million to $2 million. Did $100 by any chance come into hands in any of those years? What did you spend it on?

If there is a shocking revelation the Lord Jesus taught me in the last few years concerning becoming rich, it is that it is not dependent on how much I have. You must learn this law, believe it, and apply it. It would greatly help you. This has built my confidence over the years.

Many Christians complain today that the reason they are not financially independent is because they don't have enough. Our Lord Jesus muted those points on several occasions when He fed thousands with loaves of bread and fish. On one occasion, He fed close to 20,000 people. The men alone were 5,000. The women and children would be double at least the men count. Amazingly, He did this with only five loaves of bread and two fish. He even had 12 baskets full of leftovers (Matthew 14:13-21). Another time He fed about 15,000 if you factor in women and children with seven loaves of bread and pieces of fish (Matthew 15:36).

You may say the examples above were because it was Jesus who did them. Do not forget that He said we would do more than He did in John 14:12. *"I tell you the truth, anyone who believes in me will do the same works I have done, and even greater works, because I am going to be with the Father.*

Jesus taught me that it is never about how much you have. It is knowing what to do with what you have, and how well you are willing to apply it. Many successful business owners and entrepreneurs in our contemporary world also have proven to us that we can do a lot with just the little we have.

The founder of Spandex, a billion-dollar company, started with only $5,000. Mary Kay Ash, the founder of the cosmetic company Mary Kay worth almost $4 billion today, also started with just $5,000.[17] Michael Dell of Dell Technologies started with $1,000 and is now worth about $37 billion, according to Bloomberg.com. Let me be bold to say, cumulatively, at least $1,000 has passed through your hands before. The question is, what did you do with it?

So, what can you do? Surround yourself with information and

become a student of financial education. Before you invest in other people's ventures, invest in yourself with information about that sector. This information would determine your priority list. For example, there are some ideas that you can't bring into fruition until you have established some base. Accordingly, depending on the stage you are in life, you can determine your investment based on the rate of return, time for the return, capital required, risk, competence required, etc. There will always be many attractive investments to choose from, but without adequate preparation, they can end up being failures.

Action Item.

1. When I am tempted to splurge, I need to start practicing what I could invest the money on.

2. I need to get magazines or visit websites that provide information on investments such as www.Kiplinger.com or www.Money.com

CHAPTER 34

LAW OF RESISTANCE

> *So the Philistines filled up all of Isaac's wells with dirt.
> These were the wells that had been dug by the servants of
> his father, Abraham. Finally, Abimelech ordered Isaac to
> leave the country. "Go somewhere else," he said, "for you
> have become too powerful for us." Isaac's servants also dug
> in the Gerar Valley and discovered a well of fresh water.
> But then the shepherds from Gerar came and claimed the
> spring. "This is our water," they said, and they argued over
> it with Isaac's herdsmen. So Isaac named the well Esek
> (which means "argument"). Isaac's men then dug another
> well, but again there was a dispute over it. So Isaac named
> it Sitnah (which means "hostility"). Abandoning that one,
> Isaac moved on and dug another well..." Genesis 26:15-22.*

The Bible told us about the story of Isaac in Gerar. Isaac, if you remember, is the son of Abraham, the great patriarch who was already blessed by God and was told would be a blessing to the world. It was already predetermined. However, there was a famine that appeared to be a contradiction to this promised blessing during the time of Isaac. How is that for encouragement? You have probably been in the same place as Isaac or perhaps still there. You received a word or several words of prophecies from God, but the reality on the ground makes the prophecies seem they are mirages.

Because of the famine mentioned above, Isaac opted to go down to Egypt to weather it out just like Abraham his father did. God told him not to. He should remain in that place where there is famine. He would bless him there. Hmm... Have you been in a place where you second guess God? "But God, I could see clearly that the grass is greener over there. God, are you sure?" Isaac remained in Gerar, and God blessed him. He reaped one hundred times what he sowed. Something around 10,000%. Where is the resistance, you may ask? Wait for it.

There was initial resistance from the soil because it was a time of famine. However, the major resistance came from the Philistines, who began to envy him and started to harm all his efforts. Because he lived in a desert area, they need a reliable source of water for the family and his vast livestock empire. The Philistines envied and now began to resist him.

First, every well that his father Abraham had dug during his lifetime they filled them up with sand. So, he moved away to the valley to try reopening other wells that his father dug. Then his servants dug a well. But the Philistines came driving away his servants, claiming the well belongs to them. Still, they persisted and dug another well, but the Philistines came and claimed that as well. So, they moved on further to dig yet another well, and this time the Philistines finally gave up. Isaac called that well, Rehoboth. After he didn't give up and succeeded, God appeared to him that night to encourage him. He reiterated the promise of blessings to him again revalidating them. Not long after they dug another well again and found water.

This law is so important for any Christian or any person who wants to be financially successful. I believe this is one of the areas where many individuals are weeded out. This is where many run out of strength. This is where exhaustion sets in. Many dreams of financial independence die here. Only very few make it past this stage.

This is an important law that you must understand if you want to be rich or financially independent as a Christian. Your efforts to do so would be resisted. The bigger your dreams, the brutal the resistance would be. That is a major reason why many Christians or individuals do not become rich. They have been resisted from all sides. They have done all that could be done and still with no significant progress. Whereas, others who it seemed have not put in the hard work, determination or time seem to move forward.

Please know that you are not alone. You are not an exception. It is not ill-luck. It is a law. This is even more profound if you are a Christian. We know we have been blessed by God. However, seeing that blessing turn into tangible financial assets sometimes appears to be a contradiction. Every choice of God is the devil's target for opposition and resistance. I cannot begin to mention to you all the instances where I have been resisted to the point of giving up. No, let me correct that. In some instances, I gave up but picked it up again after encouragement from the Lord.

By the grace of God, my experience has spanned many areas of endeavors from oil and gas to real estate, e-commerce, equities (stocks), cryptocurrencies, fine arts, publishing, pre-ipo, billboard advertising, etc. One thing I can tell you is that each sector has its own resistance that must be torn down with stubborn, unyielding determination and rugged faith in God and earnest prayers.

The book you are reading is proof that it is possible to win. I won! You will win too. In fact, you are already won from God's perspective. You just now need to go through the process with that consciousness. You can compare this to buying a book you've heard about and whose end you already knew. No matter how things turned in between the chapters, you know that things are still going to end the way you knew it. It is the same with resistance. God already predetermined the end before He gave you the vision. The end is that you win. Now, go in that consciousness and face the resistance. It will eventually yield.

Action Item.

1. I need to know that I will encounter resistance during my financial journey.

2. Resistance is not proof that it is not possible.

3. I need to read about or watch how others in my field who overcame resistance.

CHAPTER 35

LAW OF PERSISTENCE & DEALING WITH FAILURE

"for though the righteous fall seven times, they rise again...," Prov. 24:16.

Some years ago, things were really horrible for me financially. I faced severe opposition. I faced lots of failures. Some business acquaintances made away with thousands of dollars in funds that I had invested with them. Some of them were supposedly Christians. It happened in different sectors. I had prayed and fasted, and nothing was working. I was not happy. It appears those who care less about God were doing well financially, and they were. I made myself at every church activity that I could serve God to the best of my ability. Those who weren't were making bank.

Then one night, the Lord saw how distressed I was and spoke to me. It was during a time of fasting and prayer. He showed me a vision. He wrote on a board in a classroom. He spelled out these words. P E R S I S T E N C E.

The fact that God has blessed us or promised us a blessing does not imply smooth sailing. Persistence and hard work is our contribution to the process. Doors won't start opening until you decide to take drastic, relentless do or die steps even at great inconvenience to you. It is at this point that you serve notice to all obstacles and hindrances that you are serious. You also impress God that you are serious about becoming wealthy. Then the obstacles would begin to give way. The ones you can't push open by yourself, He would have mercy and help you to open it. He'd even open the ones you never expected.

To be financially successful, you must count on and prepare for the possibility of having unsuccessful attempts. I prefer to use unsuccessful attempts because failure connotes a finality.

Setbacks would come in many forms. Perhaps you had decided to embark on following some of the principles in the book, for example, savings. Because this is a new habit, you will be upbeat and excited to do it. However, maybe after a few tries, you gave in to your urge and raided your savings to pay for something not worthwhile. That is okay. Don't beat yourself up too much about it. Just pick up again and continue. I have found that when I give myself permission to fail, I succeed in the long run because I already account for failure in the journey. In fact, slip up is already baked in and expected in your journey. God expects you to succeed even with your missteps. *"for though the righteous fall seven times, they rise again..." (Proverbs 24:16).*

For Peter, it was the same boat, same net, the same sea that had caught nothing that ended catching net breaking fish. Read what Michael Jordan said. *"I've missed more than 9000 shots in my career. I've lost almost 300 games. 26 times, I've been trusted to take the game-winning shot and missed. I've failed over and over and over again in my life. And that is why I succeed."*[18] I remember that Walt Disney was turned down by over 300 banks when he pitched his idea to create the Walt Disney amusement park. Yet today, the Disney parks are known worldwide and have become iconic.

You may need to persist if you are introducing an innovative way of doing business. Structures on the ground, such as government regulations, may be in the way. In some of our businesses, we faced such, and with creativity and persistence, we were successful. Many technology companies of today faced such as well. An example is the ridesharing company Uber. It faced several regulations and oppositions from governments in various cities and countries worldwide. They were deeply unfavorable to their business. Yet, the company today has come to stay and is currently worth over $60 billion.

Still, you may need to persist when someone spreads false information about your service, your product or you. That happens quite a lot, especially when starting from a small-scale business. Again, Isaac showed us that the key is to keeping digging until we get to our Rehoboth, the space that God had made for us.

Action Item.

1. I need to prepare for setbacks in my financial journey.

2. I need to know that things would not work out exactly the way I have planned them.

CHAPTER 36

LAW OF HUMILITY & GROUND ZERO

To become rich, Jesus taught me that I must be humble. I must be humble and be willing to start low if I want to be rich God's way. In fact, in my experience, God would even take you lower than your current position before He lifts you up.

Many times, even though God has given you a big dream, perhaps of being a business mogul, you would discover that He might not begin the process of your ascent with you until you are even lower than your current status. You may have to flip burgers first or work as a cleaner or be the garbage man before you get there. Many people bypass these positions and experiences as beneath them while waiting for the "big thing."

There are several biblical and contemporary examples of financially successful individuals who started small and humbly worked their way up to achieve their dreams. Take, for example,

Joseph the dreamer. Joseph's dream, as revealed to him by God, was to be a Prime Minister of a nation. This was revealed to him by God several years earlier. Though this was his dream, he had some humbling experiences and also took up some odd jobs on the way.

For starters, Joseph was a beloved son of his father. He was dotted on. He had the coat of many colors to distinguish him. However, when God put the process in motion of achieving his dream, He allowed him to be brought lower in status. He became a slave, and it was not by choice. What path is there to the palace from being a slave?

As a slave, Joseph took on several duties administering his master's household. He then went lower again below a slave. He was thrown in prison and became a prisoner. He also took on administrative duties full time and part-time dream interpreting. Though they were humbling experiences, he never lost hope. He never lost the dream and became the Prime Minister of Egypt. He didn't fall for a get-rich-quick scheme by sleeping with the boss' wife. Get-rich-quick schemes are not from God. Any business that promises unimaginable returns in no time is almost certainly guaranteed to make you lose your money. No matter how attractive it is or who is selling it, wealth building principles as outlined in the bible takes time. God does His work in time. Satan is the one that always promises instant wealth while hiding the grave dangers that lie underneath.

Starting low is not the only humbling experience you may encounter on your journey to become rich God's way. You may lose all that you have invested. It is possible that you had invested your resources before and lost all. While it is a difficult, painful experience, it is not impossible to recover from.

There was a time in the life of David when he lost all he had ever worked for and that of his company in one single day. Perhaps your retirement savings have been wiped off by a bad investment or series of terrible mistakes, divorce, and company going out of business or because of the pandemic. It is still possible to recover all with God and determination.

David sought the Lord for directions, and he recovered all (I Sam 30:8). He recovered all within a few days. Now your result may vary based on what you have lost and how long, but it is still possible to recover. Job lost everything. I mean everything, including his children and health. Over time, with God's help, he recovered twice what he lost, including his health. He lived another 140 years after recovering double, so he could enjoy them. How is that for recovery (Job 42:16-17)?

Of course, I will give a modern-day example. One of the most prime examples I love to tell is that of Apple Inc, the maker of iPhone, iPad, Macintosh computer, etc. Do you know that there was a time this company was teetering on the brink? Then Steve Jobs, the CEO, reached out to Microsoft, which was then a bigger company for investment. Microsoft invested $150 million (an amount which has since been repaid by the company), injecting new life into it.[19] The same Apple today is the most valuable company in the world by market capitalization. Apple is currently worth over $1.800 Trillion as of the time of this writing, while Microsoft is worth over $1.500 Trillion. This lets you know that where you are today does not determine where you would end.

Action Item.

1. I need to know that God always starts everyone from a humble beginning.

2. Know that things going bad for me doesn't mean my financial dreams won't happen.

3. Determine that where I am today is not where I will end.

Chapter 37

Law of Lonely Road

"The LORD had said to Abram, "Leave your native country, your relatives, and your father's family, and go to the land that I will show you. So Abram departed as the LORD had instructed..."Genesis 12:1,4.

When you plant a grain of corn in the soil, within a few days, you'd see it start sprouting. In about fifty-five days, it should reach maturation ready to eat. It is not so for a palm tree. It could appear dead for months as you would not see anything above the surface. Everything is happening underground, in the soil unseen by anyone.

For a palm tree, developing fruit ready to eat could also take years. However, it has more uses than corn and very resistant to destruction from the elements. A palm tree could provide shade, the oil could be used for cooking or ointment, the wood could be used in building a canoe or manufacturing a weapon, the shaft for fuel, it also provides a nest for birds, used as pencils, etc. No wonder the bible compares a Christian to a palm tree. *"But the godly will flourish like palm trees..."Psalm 92:12.* It takes a while for us to mature into a palm tree that is a source of blessings to those around us.

Just like the progress of the palm tree is hidden, unexciting for a while, the road to financial success and implementing sound financial principles for a Christian could also be lonely sometimes. Because many live lives that lack financial discipline, you would find yourself as one of the rare few going on this road. The road could be boring and unexciting compared to what others are doing. While some are buying new cars, getting the latest in electronic gadgets, your commitment based on the knowledge you have acquired prevents you from doing this.

As you would notice when Jesus starts taking you on the journey to becoming rich, the initial stages would be spent developing your roots, your foundation, your habits, and your center of attention. Since the progress is not above ground and flashy like others, you may feel left out. You may feel like throwing in the towel and just splurge.

When God called Abraham, He called him alone. He told him to get out of all that is familiar to the unknown. He only has the promise of a blessing to hold on to. The servants in his household were popping babies while the boss had none. In fact, 318 battle-ready men were born in his house, and he didn't have any for years. His nephew also had children, but the covenant person, Abraham is the one who didn't have a single one. However, today, that one child, Isaac, has blessed the entire world and has descendants that are still thriving thousands of years later. All others are who were not are not memorable. Jesus also wants to build enduring wealth with you if you would let Him despite the lonely road.

Sometimes, it is possible to want to give in to discouragement when you see the little you have compared to what others have accumulated. Don't be. Don't compare. We all have different races to run.

You can never give up. You must stay focused. You must not lose sight of your goal. You must always find a way to motivate yourself. There will be many temptations to hang up and throw in the towel. There will be the temptation of gratification. There will be a temptation to put all other things ahead of your goal. The champions are those who can resist the temptation and soldier on.

I can tell you that if you don't give up and stay focused. You will achieve your goal, just like exercising. It could be painful for you. Some of your painful moments would come from the fact that you are not seeing the results of what you're doing quickly well enough. Do not give up. Changes are happening even though you don't see them. There's something going on in the roots. You are doing deepening your roots for long-term growth and endurance.

Do you want a suggestion on how to weather this stage? Generally, in my Christian walk, I keep journals. Two of my most important are the Journal of Revelation and that of Answered Prayers & Psalms. My journal of revelation includes every major thing that God communicates to me. They vary from dreams to the audible voice of God, visions, etc. This has helped to keep me motivated when I am tired, and things are not working out.

The Answered Prayers & Psalms is self-explanatory. In it, I list the records of major prayers that God has answered in my life. I describe how I was feeling around the time before He came through for me. I also keep notes of major victories in this journal as well. You also need an inspirational package to keep you balanced and focused on the big picture while your roots are deepening.

Action Item.

1. I need to list my "whys" for becoming rich.

2. I need to have inspirational packages to motivate me

3. I need to have testimonial journal for my successes no matter how little.

PART VII:
INCOME
CREATING LAWS

T o become rich, you need income. In this section, I discuss how to create money from creating value. I provided specific sources of income that you could engage right away to speed up your journey to riches.

CHAPTER 38

LAW OF MULTIPLE STREAMS OF INCOME

"Invest in seven ventures, yes, in eight; you do not know what disaster may come upon the land." Ecclesiastes 11:2 NIV.

One financial law Jesus taught me is the law of multiple streams of income. I call it the scripture-backed guaranteed income recession-proof plan. If you want to become rich, you need more than one source of income. If you want to weather any economy downturn from any source, you need multiple streams of income. Did you know the Bible actually recommended this thousands of years before we came on the scene?

At the time of this writing, the world is going through a pandemic. But do you know as a Christian, if you had learned this law and applied it, you would have been fine? More likely, you would even have seen your net worth go up and not down! This law is found in the book of *Ecclesiastes 11:2 Invest in seven ventures, yes, in eight; you do not know what disaster may come upon the land. NIV.*

Did you see that? How would you have love to have seven to eight streams of income? This scripture even said you don't know what disaster may come upon the land. Essentially, it means a disaster such as the COVID-19 pandemic could leave you exposed and wipe you out if all your income is coming from only one source. Definitely, seven or eight streams of income is a buffer.

Let's put this into practice. As of this writing, if all your investments were, for example, in the airline industry, oil and gas, automobile, cruise lines or other companies that had taken a bad beating during the COVID-19 pandemic, you would have been severely impacted. However, let's say in addition to the airline industry, oil and gas, automobile, cruise lines, your source of income is also from technology companies like Amazon, Facebook, Apple and other companies like Walmart, you would have a different tale.

Fortunately, the technology age has made it easier to add multiple streams of income. Below are practical ways to earn multiples streams of income.

Disclaimer: I have no affiliation with any of the companies mentioned below. Kindly do your due diligence before investing in any venture. Also, information was current as of this writing but may have changed.

1. **Selling T- Shirts Online** - Chances are that you have at least a T-shirt in your closet. It could be of your pet, your political party, bible verse, favorite band, age etc. People buy T-shirts every day for various reasons. Why don't you be the person that would fill that void? This is one of the most relatively easy businesses to set up as long as you have a personal computer. As of this writing, the method that I am recommending doesn't you require to maintain any inventory, pay any upfront costs, process customers' payments or ship the product. Visit any of these websites and sign up. Once that is done, upload a T-shirt design to your store. It could be what you designed

yourself or have someone designed for you. Then, let people know about it via your social media page. Post the link to the page. Everything else from printing the T-shirts, shipping, processing customers' payments is handled by the printing company. Some tips for fast selling T-shirts are trending topics, religion, political parties, pets, careers, age etc. Some of the T-shirts companies you can explore are teespring.com, gearbubble.com and amazon.com. You can upload the same design to each of the companies earning multiple streams of income simultaneously.

2. **Tutoring Income** - One of the areas that I see would explode because of COVID-19 is online tutoring. Many students are forced to go to school remotely at home. Parents are also working from home in many cases. It might be too tasking for parents to combine doing homework with their children and teleworking. You can take this burden off their shoulders by signing up to tutor online. Some of the websites offering these are Chegg.com, tutor.com.

3. **Writing Income** - Have you been in a terrible situation and survived? Write about it. e.g., "How I Beat COVID-19," "How I Acquired New Skill During COVID-19," "How We Started A Thriving Business During COVID-19,"etc. The world is looking for solutions from those who are successful and would pay for them. You can also write fiction. You can do freelance writing. You can write blog content for others. You can be a ghostwriter where someone pays you to publish your work under their name. You can also self-publish as soon as you have your content together. An easy way to generate content is to always journal. When you journal regularly, you would not lack content to write about. It would make the process relatively easy. Else, you can dictate your thoughts and search for those that can transcribe it on a website such as Fiverr.com or Upwork.com The text could then be sent to some websites that offer self-publishing such as amazon.

com, bookbaby.com.

4. **Teaching or Mentorship Income** - If you know another language, have you considered teaching it online? How about cooking? Do you have ideas about how to create a healthy relationship? How about advertising? Preaching? There are at least three ways to profit from this. One of the ways could be setting up a YouTube channel where you get paid from advertisers sponsoring your page. Another way could be turning these into a course where people pay a fixed price to download this course. This could become residual income. You could also set up a personal website where you sell related merchandise to your audience.

5. **Arts & Craft Income** - If you are good with your hands, you can sell your arts and craft on websites such Etsy. com, Amazon Handmade, Turningart.com , etc.

6. **Rental Income** - You can also have income from renting out what you have control over. You can rent out a part of your home using websites such as Airbnb.com, vrbo.com, etc. In some cases, you may not necessarily own the property outright. You could sign an agreement with a landlord to manage the property and then rent out the home for short term stay to those looking for hotel-like. You could also rent out equipment camera, 3D printer, musical instrument, helium cylinder for blowing balloons, etc. You can also rent out your car, just like traditional car companies do. On one of my trips, I used this service, and the experience was fine. Some companies that offer these are Turo.com and GetAround.com. There are limitless possibilities for rental income. You can rent out used books on Chegg.com. You could also rent your land for billboard installation or the wall of your building for advertisement and earn a good income. Websites like www.outdoorbillboard.com is a great resource for this. You may also visit turningart.com to rent your fine

arts to display in buildings.

7. **Sell Old Stuff** - Do you know you can get paid for selling stuff you consider old and worthless? One person's junk is another's treasure. If you have old stuff you want to get rid of and get paid for them, sites such as Offerup, Ebay and Craigslist are some ways to do this. What you could also do is get items for free on sites like Freecycle and sell them on other sites.

8. **Dividend Income** - During the 2008 financial meltdown, many companies were looking for cash to stay afloat. One of the people that stepped forward to provide cash and made good fortunes was Warren Buffett. He invested in a handful of companies by loaning them money and in exchange for getting some equity or a portion of their business. In addition, he was also getting dividend income. It is sort of interest paid to you as a reward for owning a piece of a company. You can also have regular income from owning stocks. For example, if you own shares of Apple and other dividend-paying stocks, they pay a quarterly dividend to shareholders who own their stocks.

9. **Interest Income** – Have you ever had folks who borrowed money from you and never paid back? Well, there are more structured ways to do that and with less possible risk while making a regular income. You can make money lending your money as little as $50. Some platforms that do this are: Kiva, Prosper, Upstart, LendingClub, Funding Circle, Peerform, etc.

10. **Funny Videos** - Do you know that we use a lot of our times watching funny video clips that were either forwarded to us or that showed up on our screens? There are several folks who make money from generating funny content. I remember a story that I saw of some young boys in Africa

who pride themselves in making local scale down version of movies and popular events. There was a time they mimicked Netflix's movie the Extractor and tagged the company on Twitter. Among the props they used were some cardboards and wheelbarrow for an automobile. Netflix was greatly impressed by this and sent them all kinds of video and recording equipment set to modernize their craft.

11. **Delivery Income** - There are many platforms to use in generating income from delivery. They include Doordash, Instacart, Shipt, Postmates, Shipt, Grubhub, Minibar, GoPuff, etc.

12. **Cleaning and Disinfecting Business** - There is a high demand for cleaning due to COVID-19 in business establishments, churches, etc. You can set up a business to take advantage of this.

13. **Video Content Entertainment For Kids** - What is one thing that many parents and those working from home are looking for? How to keep their kids busy. You could start a video online to entertain kids. Ryan, a boy whose parents helped to set up a YouTube channel made over $26 million 2019. You only need a Smartphone, Light and a YouTube account.

14. **Capital Gains Income** - You can buy assets that increase in value for capital gains income. House, baseball cards, fine art, stocks, rare coins, gold chains, metals, rare stamps, rare comic books, letters of prominent figures, old arts and crafts, rare paper notes, antique products, cars are some products to consider for this.

15. **Shopify** - Shopify is an online platform to sell things. Some hot categories to sell are gym sets, pet accessories, camera accessories, toys for kids, books for kids. You can also go online to Google.com and type Google Trends into the

search box. It would let you know what people are searching for especially to purchase.

16. **Contracting Services Income - Business To Business** - You can sign up with platforms such as Field Nation, Field Engineer, Work Market and perform basic tasks for businesses. Some could be as simple as hooking up a printer.

17. **Contracting Services Income- Business To Consumer** - This is similar to the above. The only difference is that tasks are performed to consumers directly. Platforms such as Task Rabbit, Thumbtack, Zeel could be used for this. Tasks could be anything from shopping to dog walking to cleaning.

18. **Influencer Income** – The new digital economy and social media has brought with it diverse opportunities never before thought of. One source of income that is novel due to social media is income from being a social media influencer. Basically, companies and individuals could pay you to promote their products on your social media page to your followers. The amount could vary from a few hundred dollars to millions if you are Kylie Jenner or Kim Kardashian.

Action Item

1. Evaluate my current sources of income. I'm I prepared for a disaster?

2. Review the figure below for at least 150 streams of income.

3. I need to start working on at one least one source of income in the next four weeks.

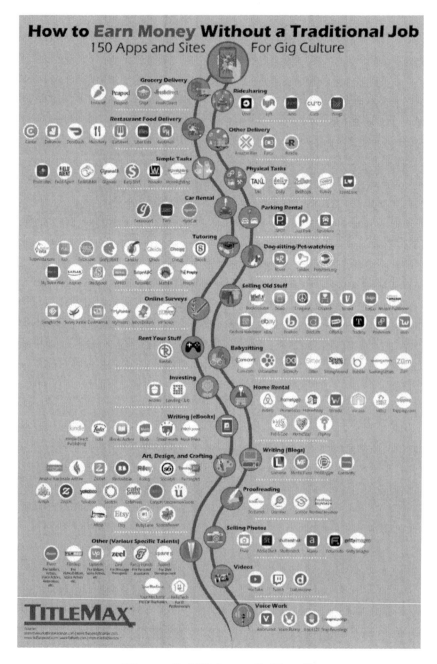

Figure 5. 150 Apps & Sites.[20]

CHAPTER 39

LAW OF MONETIZING YOUR SKILLS & HOBBIES

"as His divine power has given to us all things that pertain to life and godliness..."2 Peter 1:3 KJV.

In the last chapter I listed some of what you could do get additional sources of income. It's possible you may find any of them appealing. That is why I wrote this chapter. I want to tell you about other means of additional income. Some are within you or within your reach.

If you are like me, many of the things that I do with ease, I don't usually put a premium on them. I even sell myself short when others commend me on certain intuitive skills that I execute with ease to solve some problems, which they could not do. I see this happen to other people as well.

Because we possess some innate skills to perform some tasks excellently well, we do not think too much of them. Most of the time we do them for free for everyone who requests for them. We also tend not to think anything of them because they are not our main source of income. Were they to be our main source of income, we would probably not downplay them. Yet, we see many people monetizing their skills and having financial independence off of them.

For example, may be you can cook up a storm. People like your food. They enjoy it. However, because it's not your accounting job or human resources career, you never thought of getting compensated for the services you render. Of course, I am not saying that you charge for everything and be money hungry. You can do it for free if the situation warrants it. However, I want you to look at your skills with a different perspective from now.

One of the truths that Jesus taught me about becoming rich is using my knowledge, skills and talents. He made me realize that God gave me these skills and talents not only to serve others but to be compensated for using them. He asked me whether I could go to an accountant who uses their accounting skills and ask them to do my books for free? I said no. He said that is how I should view my skills, talents and abilities.

What I am saying is that there are hobbies, skills and talents that God has given you that you can monetize. When you look at the individuals that we cheer today, earning the biggest amount of money, it is not because they cured some great illnesses plaguing mankind or provided answers to the world's greatest problems. It is because they have monetized their hobbies. For example, Michael Jordan monetized playing basketball and is now the first billionaire athlete. Oprah, who monetized talking to people is also a billionaire. Countless musicians have monetized their musical talents and are doing very well.

Our heavenly Father has endowed everyone with the gifts and skills to succeed in life. Those who use them successfully become financially independent. Some have monetized their ability to paint, repair, etc. I ask you, what skills do you have? What do you do well that others commend you for? Monetize them.

Our talents, skills and abilities often get the cold shoulder from us. They are not the big, spectacular skills and abilities we desire compared to what others have. Even so, do you know God gave us those abilities to profit from them?

Perhaps, you've been like me and other Christians who had cried many times to God for more financial breakthrough? But God is saying to you and me like He said to Moses at the Red Sea. "Why are you crying to me? Stretch your talents and gifts and monetize them to make a way for you." Do you know how to organize, why not start getting compensated for it instead of doing it pro bono every time?

Your skills, talents and abilities should be monetized as one of your streams of income. This is one of the law of becoming rich that Jesus revealed to me. Let me be more practical. For example, do you know people in strategic places? Do you know buyers and sellers on opposite end of transactions, you could offer a flat fee or percentages for facilitating the connection to create referral income. This is a norm in many industries. They call them brokers. I have used this method to generate income for myself. Maybe that is not for you. Have people commended you about how lovely your voice is? You can do voice work. In fact, I recently paid someone with a nice voice, who is a member of my church to record the voice message at one of our online companies. There are thousands of individuals looking for this service as well. You may register at Fiverr.com and list yourself as available. In one of the action items below, you would find a Pastor who made $1.5 million monetizing his voice.

What gifts and ideas are you going to work on and deploy to serve God's other children? God is not a respect of persons. The bible tells us Jew and Gentile are the same in this respect. They have the same Lord, who gives generously to all who call on him. Romans 10:12.

Action Item

1. Take an inventory of my talents, skill and abilities.

2. Visit https://www.cnbc.com/2018/04/24/how-this-dad-made-almost-1-million-on-fiverr.html and read this story of this Pastor who made $1.5 million monetizing his voice.

3. Visit Fiverr.com & Upwork.com to explore how to list and monetize the skills that I have.

Chapter 40

Law of Earning While Sleeping

"It's useless to rise early and go to bed late, and work your worried fingers to the bone. Don't you know he enjoys giving rest to those he loves?" Psalm 127:2.

One of the principles or laws that Jesus taught me for becoming rich is the law of earning while sleeping. Could you imagine while you were sleeping if someone had placed an order for your product, paid for your service, and you have not even brushed your teeth?

When my wife and I started a clothing apparel company I remembered the day we started making sales. I was ecstatic. It was overnight. It was even on a Sunday. I never had anything to do with beyond designing and listing it at our online store. The manufacturer did the work of printing, taking the money and shipping it to the customer. It was sweet.

If the only time you have to earn money is when you awake, it might take a while before you become rich or attain financial independence. You need to put a system in place where money continuously flows to you without repeatedly working for it. There are so many choices available to do this, especially with the explosion of the App or online economy. You could write a book. You could develop a course. Those interested would pay for it around the world whether you are awake or not. I have paid thousands of dollars for courses online, and I have never met the author before.

Another way you can while sleeping could also be investing in other companies through stocks. I personally view this as hiring people to go to work for me for a fraction of what they would normally earn. Because you have invested in that company, whatever they earn is part of what you earn as well.

Action Item.

1. What system could I introduce into my current source of income to earn while I sleep?

2. What other business venture can I start to earn while sleeping?

CHAPTER 41

LAW OF CREATING VALUE

""And you shall remember the Lord your God, for it is He who gives you power to get wealth..."Deuteronomy 8:18. NKJV.

I f you looked at the above scripture verse, it tells us what God gives us regarding wealth. God does not rain down dollars or other currencies to Christians who are in covenant relationship with Him. He gives them the power, which could be interpreted as ability, ideas, and resources to get money that makes them rich and wealthy.

One of the favorite prosperity scriptures for Christians is the wealth transfer scripture found in proverbs 13:22. *"...but the sinner's wealth passes to the godly."* I remember that as a young boy growing up, I used to picture in my mind's eye an actual transfer from the bank accounts of ungodly people into our accounts as Christians. I am sure some Christians also hold this view. As I mature in the Lord, I knew that was not what He has in mind for His children as the method to make them rich.

Jesus taught me that creating value is what creates money. Money is what you get when you create value, whether it is monetized or not. What God gives us is the ability to create value, which then gives us wealth. To be rich, create value. Monetize that value and then serve or present it to those who would pay you for it. The more people you serve with it, the more money you should have.

When Microsoft created Windows '95 and launched it, it was a blockbuster product that served billions around the world. Billions of people find it valuable and paid for it. The company made more money and profited greatly. This increased the net worth of the founders in billions of dollars. Then more people thought, we see value in this company. We will buy a piece of it via stock investment to own a piece of the company. This increased the value of the company and the net worth of the founders and directors even further.

Let me give you one practical example. I told my wife one day that it is easy to make money. All you need to do is create value. I put the principle of creating value to test. I went on a website called Teespring.com, which I mentioned under Law of Multiple Sources of Income and created a T-shirt. I actually created a design. They already have the T-shirts. I uploaded my design to the T-shirt. I then posted the link to where it is to my followers on Facebook, who I know buy T-shirts with Christianity inscriptions. They bought several.

As an author, I also create value when I put years of tested principles or my experiences in print for people who can identify with them. It solves a problem for them. They can avoid pitfalls. For some, it might be the humor they need to bring them out of the funk they are currently in. Just like they would give money in exchange for services provided by a plumber, they also pay for the solution provided in the book.

You can also do something similar or more. If many people have commented on how excellent your cooking is, you can start making some of your signature meals for sale. If you have a heart-tugging story that people always want to hear, why don't you put it into a book to bless someone else going through the same?

But, you can't create value until you have invested in yourself. Read the law of investing in yourself for more information.

Action Item.

1. I need to think of where I can create value.

2. I need to look at suggestions under the Law Of Multiple Streams of Income.

CHAPTER 42

LAW OF EMBRACING TECHNOLOGY

> *"And no one puts new wine into old wineskins. For the wine would burst the wineskins, and the wine and the skins would both be lost. New wine calls for new wineskins." Mark 2:22*

There is no shortcut to wealth. Any perceived shortcut would only result in losses, pains, heartaches or even jail. The bible tells us in Proverbs 21:5 *Good planning and hard work lead to prosperity, but hasty shortcuts lead to poverty.* Looking for hasty shortcuts is one of the symptoms of those craving money referred to in I Timothy 6:7. *"... And some people, **craving money,** have wandered from the true faith and pierced themselves with many sorrows."*

Though there is no shortcut to wealth, however, you can and should shorten your time frame for becoming financially independent. I will go into detail in a bit. But first, you should remember that you only have a fixed period of time allocated to you by God to accomplish the purpose for which He had sent you into the world. Once the time is up, you depart. That is why Moses wrote in Psalms 90:14, *Oh, satisfy us early with Your mercy, that we may rejoice and be glad all our days! NKJV*.

In addition to the fixed time period to live, it is also better to attain financial independence early or shorten that time frame so that you will be able to drive the vision while still young, strong and healthy. What good is having your first gourmet meal when you've lost all your teeth at 90 years of age? When you grow older, there would be so many things you would desire to do, which your health won't be able to support. Just imagine if King David had to be fighting battles into his 60s? He would have spent his entire lifetime fighting battles because he died at 70 years of age.

One of the secrets, let me say major secret Jesus taught me for shortening the time to becoming rich is to embrace technology and especially emerging technology. In fact, in a live show called *Jesus Is Too Real* that I host on Facebook and Instagram with the same name every Thursday, I mentioned strongly that Jesus was telling everyone to embrace technology. I said this on the November 21st, 2019 edition. By January of 2020, everyone and everything was migrating online because of the Coronavirus pandemic. Let me give you some historical perspective to drive this point home. We will consider the examples of how long it took some notable historical figures to become wealthy.

In 1870, John D. Rockefeller founded Standard Oil Company. In 1916, John D. Rockefeller became America's first billionaire. That is a space of 46 years. He was born in 1839. That meant he became a billionaire at the age of 77[21]. Fortunately for him, he lived 21 more years and died at 98. He had hoped to live to be 100.

You are probably familiar with the Oracle of Omaha, Warren Buffett. He is called the world's greatest investor. This is rightly so at a massive net worth of $86 billion as of this writing. Buffett took over his flagship company Berkshire Hathaway in 1965 and became a billionaire 20 years later in 1985 at the age of 55 years. Buffett is still alive and kicking 35 years after he made his first billion.[22]

Bill Gates, who along with others, founded Microsoft in 1975, became a billionaire in 1987 at the age of 31. That was 12 years after he founded the company. He was the youngest person at the time to become a billionaire, not through an inheritance.

I will skip others and leap forward to the founder of Facebook, the largest social media platform in the world, Mark Zuckerberg. He founded Facebook in 2004. Four years later, he became a billionaire at the age of 23.[23]

Finally, the youngest billionaire who attained this status not due to inheritance, according to Forbes magazine, is Kylie Jenner. She entered the nine-digit club at the age of 21, barely three years after she started her company.[24]

There are many trends to observe from all the examples that I gave, but I will limit the points we extract. First, if you observed, the age which they all became billionaires had shrunk significantly from 77 for Rockefeller to 21 for Jenner. It kept reducing along the way. Also, the waiting period for joining the billionaire club was also compressed from 46 years for the first billionaire to three years for Jenner, the current youngest. The major factor responsible for this is embracing new and emerging technology.

Bill Gates blazed the trail into personal computing with Microsoft, and he became wealthy and everyone who embraced the technology along with him. Kylie Jenner had no physical store when she launched her Lip Kit cosmetics line on social media. Yet, within 18 months, the company made $420 million in sales, and she only has seven full-time and five part-time employees. This achievement, certainly, at a minimum, has turned the business model of old upside down. She was able to shorten the time it would take to become wealthy significantly by embracing and working a new economy prompted by new technology.

I would recommend that regardless of how you earn your current income, look into how technology could be leveraged to cut costs and give you an edge. You will be surprised that a technological solution might have been built already for your business. The following quote was attributed to the founder of Digital Equipment Corporation in 1977, *"There is no reason anyone would want a computer in their home."* I wished he was alive now and see how the personal computer has turned our world upside down. In fact, it is constantly challenging our old way of engagement and commerce. Even the future of money is being rocked with the advent of cryptocurrencies.

Of course, not all emerging technologies would succeed. There will be so many. Some are so far ahead of their time that it is not wise to invest in them. Others would just not succeed because they are pipe dreams. Still, some are just fraudulent gimmicks to make people part with their money and finance the riotous and luxury lifestyles of the management. So, how do you tell which is which and what?

First, I would recommend that you become deliberately familiar with reading either in newspapers, magazines or online articles about new technologies. If you are interested in investing in emerging technology, I will recommend that you start reading about companies that notable venture capitalists are investing in. Venture Capitalists are investors that provide capital to companies showing high growth potential in exchange for a stake in that company. Techcrunch.com and Crunchbase.com are some of the websites you may read news about new technologies from. I have no affiliation with any of the companies that I mention in this book. Only for informational purposes.

Next, you may start attending conferences that also relate to this. This would allow you to have exposure to many of these ideas that are currently being worked on. This step would make the next step a bit seamless.

Because I have a foothold in e-commerce, I know firsthand how powerful online earning potential can be. I have also come across young men and women as young as 17 years old, earning $800,000 monthly selling products in their online stores consistently. See the figure below for example. Also, an online store, a lifestyle apparel company, called Gymshark started small but is now currently worth over $1.3 billion.[25] The picture on the following page is actual snapshot of an online store's revenue.

Action Item.

1. Evaluate my business operations to see where I could incorporate technology.

2. Visit techcrunch.com and crunchbase.com for news on emerging technologies.

3. Ask Jesus to direct me on where to invest.

4. Visit Shopify.com to open an online store if electronic commerce is for me

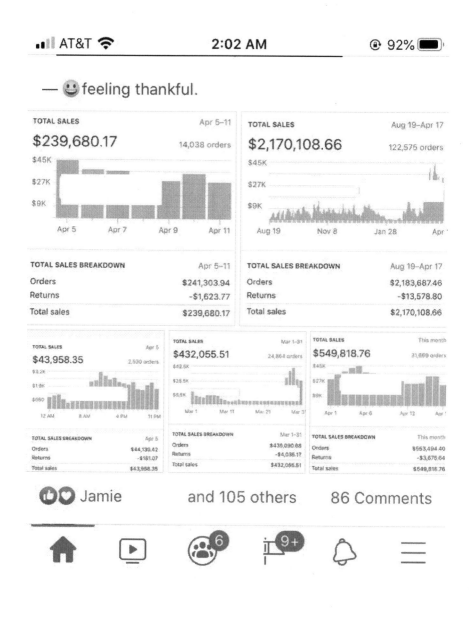

Figure 6. An Online Store Using Shopify Platform

CONCLUSION

My hope is that this book in your hands would make you prosper financially and physically as you already prospered spiritually. I want you to become rich. That is my chief joy! I have tasted and experienced the pain of living in poverty as a Christian. I have also enjoyed financial independence. I prefer the latter.

Even so, despite my aspirations for you, nothing happens till you take action. You can't take action until there is enough pain that creates positive desperation for the better. The attraction of what is ahead should motivate you to change. I want you to know that it is possible with God.

Not every venture is for you. There would be many businesses and professions that you may notice that others such as family, friends and acquaintances do successfully. This may not be for you no matter how hard you try. I have been there. Pray for divine direction. Settle on one and take massive action.

I want to see committed Christians in the top 10 ranked richest people in the world within the next 10 years. Let us change that narrative. Go ahead and acquire the top secular media houses. Buy out the top fashion houses. Take over Wall Street and Main Street. Become RICH!

*   *   *

*First of all, thank you for purchasing this book **What Did You Think of 42 Financial Independence Laws For Christians -What Jesus Taught Me On Becoming Rich During COVID-19 & Beyond?***

I know you could have picked any number of books to read, but you picked this book and for that I am extremely grateful.

If you enjoyed this book and found some benefit in reading this, I'd like to hear from you and hope that you could take some time to post a review on **Amazon**. Your feedback and support will help this author to greatly improve his writing craft for future projects and make this book even better.

I want you, the reader, to know that your review is very important and so, if you'd like to **leave a review**, all you have to do is click **here** and away you go. I wish you all the best in your future success!

I hope that it added at value and quality to your everyday life. If so, it would be really nice if you could share this book with your friends and family by posting to **_Facebook_** and **_Instagram_**.

REFERENCES

Endnotes

1 https://www.visualcapitalist.com/jeff-bezos-empire-chart/

2 Murphy Jr., Bill. *"Bill Gates Says This 1 Insane Habit Separates Highly Successful People From Everyone Else."* June 26, 2019. Inc. https://www.inc.com/bill-murphy-jr/bill-gates-vacation-weekend-microsoft-success.html Retrieved September 7, 2020.

3 Huddleston Jr., Tom. *"Jeff Bezos: Making this 1 choice is the key to success."* February 21, 2019. https://www.cnbc.com/2019/02/20/amazon-ceo-jeff-bezos-this-choice-is-the-key-to-success.html Retrieved September 7, 2020.

4 Pritchard, Ray. *"Hard Work: The Reason We Get Out of Bed."* September 4, 1994. Keep Believing Ministries. http://www.keepbelieving.com/sermon/hard-work-the-reason-we-get-out-of-bed/ Retrieved February 21, 2019

5 Mediumsizedfamily.com

6 Goldschein, Eric. Feloni, Richard. *"12 Immigrants Who Came To America With Nothing And Made A Fortune."* February 25, 2014. Business Insider. https://www.businessinsider.com/american-dream-immigrants-made-a-fortune-in-the-us-2014-2#jerry-yang-founder-of-yahoo-12 Retrieved September 15, 2020.

7 Montag, Ali. *"How this business owner landed a job at Berkshire Hathaway from Warren Buffett's famous charity lunch."* May 22, 2018. https://www.cnbc.com/2018/05/22/ted-weschler-got-job-at-berkshire-via-warren-buffetts-glide-auction.html. September 16, 2020.

8 Amaro, Silvia & Wang, Christine. *"EU leaders reach $2 trillion deal on recovery plan after marathon summit."* July 20, 2020. https://www.cnbc.com/2020/07/21/eu-leaders-reach-a-breakthrough-on-the-regions-recovery-fund.html Retrieved September 14, 2020.

9 Routley, Nick. *"The Anatomy of the $2 Trillion COVID-19 Stimulus Bill."* March 30, 2020. https://www.visualcapitalist.com/the-anatomy-of-the-2-trillion-covid-19-stimulus-bill/ Retrieved September 14, 2020.

10 Ibid.

11 Pogrebin, Robin. Reyburn, Scott. *"A Basquiat Sells for 'Mind-Blowing' $110.5 Million at Auction."* May 28, 2017. The New York Times. https://www.nytimes.com/2017/05/18/arts/jean-michel-basquiat-painting-is-sold-for-110-million-at-auction.html?_r=0 Retrieved May 28, 2017.

12 Ibid.

13 Reiley, Laura. *"Why Chick-Fil-A Is Thriving."* The Washington Post. June 19, 2019. *https://www.washingtonpost.com/business/2019/06/19/ chick-fil-a-becomes-third-largest-restaurant-chain-us/ Retrieved June 19, 2019.*

14 Ibid.

15 *The Purpose Driven Life. Retrieved September 14th, 2020.* https:// en.wikipedia.org/wiki/The_Purpose_Driven_Life

16 Blackhurst, Rob. *"Mass Appeal, The secret to Rick Warren's success."* August 14, 2011. https://slate.com/human-interest/2011/08/how-rick-warren-made-it-big.html Retrieved September 14th, 2020.

17 *"Our Founder."* Mary Kay. https://www.marykay.com/en-us/ about-mary-kay/our-founder. Retrieved September 4, 2020.

18 https://www.brainyquote.com/quotes/quotes/m/ michaeljor127660.html

19 Abell, John C. *"Aug. 6, 1997: Apple Rescued — by Microsoft."* WIRED. August 6, 2009. https://www.wired.com/2009/08/dayintech_0806/ Retrieved September 18, 2020

20 https://www.visualcapitalist.com/150-apps-power-gig-economy/

21 Ogle-mater, Janet. *"Biography of John D. Rockefeller, America's First Billionaire."* https://www.thoughtco.com/john-d-rockefeller-p2-1779821 retrieved June 10, 2019.

22 *Fiorillo, Steve.* - https://www.thestreet.com/lifestyle/warren-buffett-net-worth-14681472 retrieved June 10, 2019.

23 Elkins, Kathleen and Rogers Nicole Taylor. August 10, 2020.

"How old 14 of the world's richest people were when they first became billionaires" https://www.businessinsider.com/how-old-billionaires-were-when-they-earned-their-first-billion-2016-2#-3 Retrieved June 10/2019

24 Robehmed, Natalie. https://www.forbes.com/sites/natalierobehmed/2019/03/05/at-21-kylie-jenner-becomes-the-youngest-self-made-billionaire-ever/#2261b9f82794 Retrieved June 10/2019

25 https://www.forbes.com/sites/jodiecook/2020/08/17/how-gymshark-became-a-13bn-brand-and-what-we-can-learn/#70daffcf76ed

ABOUT THE AUTHOR

Ola Abina is the host of Jesus Is Too Real, a live program on Facebook and Instagram that uses the name and the principles of Jesus to solve contemporary problems. He also the author of *Save Me From This Hour: How To Face Life's Adversities & Come Out Stronger*. He is a kingdom financier whose business, career and investment experience spans IT, oil and gas, billboard advertising, real estate, fine art, ecommerce, IPO, equities, cryptocurrency, publishing, etc. Ola's life is saturated by a pursuit of worship, prayer and the studying of the Bible. Because of his passionate pursuit of Jesus, the Lord has visited him several times, giving him instructions and revealing to him things past, present and future. Consequently, his life's pursuit is to bring 1,000,000 individuals every year into a personal relationship with Jesus Christ. His ministry is marked with several manifestations of the Spirit, including a strong prophetic unction with accuracy, including specific names, numbers, countries, etc. He and his wife Odalisa live in Maryland with their four children.

Made in the USA
Middletown, DE
20 May 2023

30999516R00121